"Thou son of man, shew the house to the house...."

Ezekiel 43:10

Show the House to the House

VERNON L. FOWLER

SHOW THE HOUSE TO THE HOUSE
First Edition: Copyright © 2012 by Vernon L. Fowler
Expanded Edition: Copyright © 2024 by Vernon L. Fowler

This book or parts thereof may not be reproduced in any form, stored in a retrieval system, or transmitted in any form by any means — electronic, mechanical, photocopy, recording, or otherwise — without prior written permission of the author.

Unless otherwise noted, all Scripture quotations are from the King James Version (KJV) of the Bible.

Scripture quotations taken from the Amplified® Bible (AMP), Copyright © 2015 by The Lockman Foundation. Used by permission. lockman.org

Scripture quotations taken from the Amplified® Bible (AMPC), Copyright © 1954, 1958, 1962, 1964, 1965, 1987 by The Lockman Foundation. Used by permission. lockman.org.

Scripture quotations take from the (CEB) COMMON ENGLISH BIBLE. © Copyright 2011 COMMON ENGLISH BIBLE. All rights reserved. Used by permission. (www.CommonEnglishBible.com).

Scripture quotations taken from the (NASB®) New American Standard Bible®, Copyright © 1960, 1971, 1977, 1995, 2020 by The Lockman Foundation. Used by permission. All rights reserved. lockman.org

Scriptures taken from the Holy Bible, New International Version®, NIV®. Copyright © 1973, 1978, 1984, 2011 by Biblica, Inc.™ Used by permission of Zondervan. All rights reserved worldwide. www.zondervan.com The "NIV" and "New International Version" are trademarks registered in the United States Patent and Trademark Office by Biblica, Inc.™

Scripture quotations marked (NLT) are taken from the Holy Bible, New Living Translation, copyright ©1996, 2004, 2015 by Tyndale House Foundation. Used by permission of Tyndale House Publishers, Carol Stream, Illinois 60188. All rights reserved.

Abraham's Ink Publishing House
www.abrahamsinph.com

Print ISBN 979-8-9916534-8-0
Digital ISBN 979-8-9916534-1-1

Dedication

I dedicate this book to honor my spiritual father, mentor, model, motivator and minister,
Apostle Nate Holcomb,
*who has been promoted to Heaven.
You influenced countless people in your short time here on earth. I miss you more than words can truly express. I long for and look forward to the day we meet again in God's Glory!*

Acknowledgments

I want to take this opportunity to extend my sincerest thanks to my fellow partners, family, and friends, without whom this book would not be possible.

To Tracy, my wife for life, the queen of my dreams, my love and dove, my friend to the end, and the apple of my eyes: Thank you for 37 years of bliss. My heart is to someday stand before God and say, "Lord, You gave me one wife, and here is the one you gave me."

To my darling children (VJ, Angelica, Shara, and Charity): I am absolutely proud of all four of you. As tough as I have been as a father, friend, and pastor, you all have remained courteous, respectful, and totally supportive of me all these years.

To all the faithful members of my congregation at Dominion: you all know you are the "best'est" congregation any pastor could ever have. I love you, guys and gals. We are family!

To all the Bring the Book (BTB) Ministry partners: Thank you so much for your fervent prayers, fellowship, and financial support that enables me to let down the nets and bring in the great harvest of souls.

Finally, to the late Apostle Nate and Pastor Valerie Holcomb: I cannot thank you enough for the teaching, counsel, mentorship, love, and friendship. I accredit most of what is written in this book to your teaching. You really are Mom and Dad to me. Love you both.

Table of Contents

Introduction 9

1. The Lord's House.. 11
2. The Pattern of the House 21
3. The Form of the House 57
4. The Fashion of the House 87
5. The Unity of the House 93
6. The Treasury of the House 107
7. The Healthy Church 123
8. The Holy Spirit's Ministry 131
9. The Father's Anointing 145
10. The Mighty Hand of God 153

About the Author 167

Vernon L. Fowler

Introduction

"Thou son of man, shew the house to the house of Israel, that they may be ashamed of their iniquities: and let them measure the pattern."

Ezekiel 43:10 (KJV)

The purpose of this book is to show people what the House of the Living God (more intimately known as the Church) should look like and how it should function, according to God's intended purpose, as outlined in the Holy Scriptures. This book is not written from a denominational or religious perspective. It has been written according to the revelation that comes from the Father, under the inspiration of the Holy Spirit, and with the manifestation of Jesus Christ on every page.

This is not meant to be an exhaustive study but a mere "snapshot" of the pattern (dimensions), form (foundation), and fashion (structure) required for any church to be considered the "Lord's House." Just as the Lord carried Ezekiel in the Spirit and revealed the place of His throne and the glory of His dwelling place, the Lord has pulled back the "curtains of my mind" and imparted the contents of this book over the course of over 25 years.

I want to point out that I do not consider anything I have shared a private interpretation. Much of what I have written came by way of the teachings of my "father in the faith," the late Apostle Nate Holcomb. Additionally, I have spent considerable time in prayer and study to receive the intimate revelation for myself. In other words, my Apostle milked the cow, but I churned my own butter!

I pray that everyone reading this book will prayerfully allow the Holy Spirit to reveal the heart of the Father, as outlined in the book of Ezekiel, Chapter 43, and allow Him to "Show the House to the House."

The Lord's House 1

"Unless the Lord builds the house,
the builders labor in vain"
PSALM 127:1 THE LIVING BIBLE

After Jacob escaped from his brother Esau, he came to a certain place and lay asleep upon one of the stones from that place; he dreamed a dream of a ladder set up on the earth and reached heaven with the angels of God ascending and descending on it. The LORD stood above it and spoke to Him. When he awoke, he said, "Surely the Lord is in this place, and I did not know it. He was afraid and said, How to be feared and reverenced is this place! This is none other than the house of God, and this is the gateway to heaven" (Genesis 28:16-17 AMPC)! Right from the outset, the Lord intended His house to be an awesome place where people would come and reverence Him. For this reason, He required painstaking detail in establishing His dwelling place and will accept nothing less than mastery from the builders.

The specificity of design and detail of function has always been supplied by the Lord, all the way back to the exodus from Egypt, the construction of the Tabernacle, and the building of the temple in the Old Testament. Even more, the Lord has made it crystal clear concerning the building of His House. Psalms 127:1a says, "Except the LORD build the house (definite article), they labour in vain that build it…." The inference is that except the house of God is built according to the exact design and the specifications provided by the Lord, the builders are wasting time.

For example, if I was to hire someone to build a house for me, I would first have to approve the blueprints before starting the project. Once approved, the builders would be allowed to begin construction according to the approved plans. I would then visit the house periodically to ensure it is built to my specifications. Any deviations or changes require my consent. Upon completion of the house and prior to my approval of the final product, I will inspect the house to see if it has been built according to the original plans. If not, I will not agree to make payment because it does not meet my intent and is, therefore, not "my house."

This is precisely what the Lord is delineating in Psalm 127. He will not endorse a house built contrary to His original plans, and therefore, He will not move in! This also means that He will not provide the protection, provision, or financial support for a house that does not meet His approval—it is simply a waste of time. Moreover, in John 16:18, Jesus declares, "Upon this rock, I will build my church," establishing that He is the builder of His house. Although it is understood that church in this context comes from the Greek word *ekklesia*, which bespeaks of the people, most of us will agree that Jesus is also announcing that He is the builder of the place we call the House of God.

I am not saying that we have to have a physical building to be the church, but I am saying that a place of assembly has always been the heart of our Heavenly Father. Therefore, I intend to explicate the exact pattern, form, and fashion of the Lord's House according to the detailed plans outlined in the Scriptures.

The Tabernacle

> "And let them make me a sanctuary; that I may dwell among them. According to all that I shew thee, after the pattern of the Tabernacle, and the pattern of all the instruments thereof, even so shall ye make it."
> EXODUS 25:8-9 (KJV)

When God delivered His people from Egypt, which is a type of the world, His first order of business was to give them leadership, laws to live by, and a place to assemble together to meet with Him. According to Exodus 25, this place was called the Tabernacle, a temporary dwelling place where the Ark of the Covenant was to be kept. While I will not address the Ark in detail, it is important to point out that it represented the presence of the Lord in the House of God. The Ark was a symbol of the Lord dwelling among His people.

What stands out from the beginning is that God did not allow Moses and the people to build what they thought was best for Him. In Exodus, Chapters 25 through 27, God gave explicit instructions concerning the design and functions of His dwelling place. The Lord was precise and very strict as it related to the pattern of the Tabernacle and all the instruments to be utilized therein. Furthermore, from Exodus, Chapters 28 through 30, He directed Moses to outline—down to the minutest detail—the functions in the Tabernacle and the garments of those that would minister as the holy priesthood. He even instructed Moses concerning preparation prior to their operation in the Tabernacle.

It is recorded in Exodus 39:43 that "Moses did look upon all the work, and, behold, they had done it as the LORD had commanded, even so had they done it: and Moses blessed them." Moses was required to inspect the Tabernacle, the Ark, and all of the instruments to ensure that they met the detailed specifications of the Lord. Once approved, the Scripture says in Exodus 40:34, "Then a cloud covered the tent of the congregation, and the glory of the Lord filled the tabernacle." This was the first reference to the house that God built!

Solomon's Temple

> "... *See now, I dwell in an house of cedar, but the ark of God dwelleth within curtains.*"
>
> 2 Samuel 7:2 (KJV)

In the Book of 2 Samuel, Chapter 7, the Scriptures record that after David had been given rest from all his enemies, he surveyed his house and all of the blessings God had bestowed upon him. He then began to express to Nathan, the prophet, how displeased he was with the fact that the Lord had blessed him with a house of cedar while the Ark was located in a tent. Nathan began to encourage David that the Lord had placed this in his heart. The Lord then gave Nathan a Word for David: He would allow his seed to build a house for His name's sake and the throne of his kingdom forever. This blessed David so much that the Scripture says of David, "Moreover, because I have set my affection to the house of my God, I have of mine own proper good, of gold and silver, which I have given to the house of my God, over and above all that I have prepared for the holy house" (1 Chronicles 29:3).

There is no doubt that David understood that the Lord's house would require specific standards and specifications; even though it would be his son Solomon who would ultimately build this house, David spared no expense to ensure that it would be built at the highest levels of excellence. After the death of David, Solomon set out to build the house of the Lord, and once again, he had to wait for the specific plans from God. Second Chronicles 3:3 records, "Now these are the things wherein Solomon was instructed for the building of the house of God." Just as God orchestrated the Tabernacle, so he would construct this edifice.

When the house was finished, Solomon brought in all the things his father provided and assembled all the elders and priests for the building dedication service. The house must have met God's approval because 2 Chronicles 7:1 records, "Now when Solomon had made an end of praying, the fire came down from heaven, and consumed the burnt offering and the sacrifices; and the glory of the Lord filled the house." The Lord then promised them that as long as they functioned as required and made prayer a top priority, His presence would be in this house forever (Verse 16). In other words, the Lord is committed to the house built to His standards; thus, He will provide protection, provision, and financial support because, after all, it is His House!

A Holy House

> "Your testimonies are fully confirmed; holiness befits your house, O Lord forevermore."
> Psalm 93:5 (NASB 1995)

The Lord's House

"...holiness adorns your house for endless days, O Lord."

Psalm 93:5b (NIV)

Holiness is the one attribute that makes God's house uniquely different from every other place. In Leviticus 20:7, God says, "Be ye holy, for I am holy." The word *holy* bespeaks the purity of God's character. This is why He is called the Holy One. What's more, our holiness signifies sanctification or separation from sin unto God in terms of character and conduct.

God is pure and righteous in nature and all of His ways. He will, therefore, not accept anything less than absolute holiness (purity) when it comes to His house. For this reason, the Lord commands the priesthood in Leviticus 10:10, "And that ye may put difference between holy and unholy," and under no circumstances will the Lord compromise this standard. Moses, David, and Solomon all understood that holiness was an essential element in ensuring the Lord would be pleased with His house. Paul articulated this by saying, "Follow peace with all men, and holiness, without which no man shall see the Lord" (Hebrews 12:14).

It is important to note that holiness is not a denomination, as some have asserted, and it is not what we wear or how we look. The holiness of God connotes His character as reflected by yielding to His Spirit and allowing the Spirit's fruit to flow through and in our conduct. This is what Jesus was alluding to in the "Be-attitudes" when

He declared, "Blessed are the pure (holy) in heart: for they shall see God" (Matthew 5:8). Lastly, speaking through the prophet Malachi, the Lord affirms, "For I am the Lord, I change not" (Malachi 3:6).

That brings us to Ezekiel, Chapter 43, where the Spirit of the Lord reveals to the prophet that Israel defiled the house of the Lord with whoredom, idolatry, and other iniquities.

Furthermore, the people of God strayed away from the pattern, commandments, and ordinances required in determining the suitability of the Lord's dwelling place. The bottom line is our God is the same yesterday, today, and forevermore! Thus, He will never change His expectations or standards of conduct, especially where the building of His house is concerned. He was, still is, and will always be a holy and righteous God who will accept nothing less for His house.

A House of Prayer

> *"It is written, My house is the house of prayer:*
> *but ye have made it a den of thieves."*
> Luke 9:46 (KJV)

Notice, in every biblical reference, God provided the detailed blueprints for His house through the vehicle of prayer. For example, Moses went to the Mount to speak to God face to face to get the details for the Tabernacle. When Solomon prayed, the Lord gave him the design for the temple. While in the Spirit, Ezekiel heard the voice of the Lord speaking to him concerning the pattern of His house. Finally, because Jesus said, "My house shall be called the house of prayer" (Mark 11:17), there is no way to begin to build or maintain the House of the Lord without prayer. In prayer, the Holy Spirit can provide the wisdom and revelation of the details, timing, and place for the building of the Lord's house.

Prayer is the critical element that cannot be compromised for any reason. In prayer, we first receive the vision of God to see what God wants clearly, capture the heart of God for the passion and faith to build, and hear the voice of God for specific instructions. This is why Jesus said to His disciples, "When ye pray, say, Thy kingdom come, Thy will be done, as in heaven, so in earth" (Luke 11:2). The Lord wants to reveal His will or what He wants, as it relates to the building and functioning of His house.

By prayer, we ensure the church is not what Jesus called a "den of thieves or house of merchandise." Coincidently, we may be able to say that we are doing a lot of "good things," but if we are not doing the primary thing, and that is praying, we are robbing God of His opportunity to get the glory in the earth. Thus, we have made His house a robber's den. Prayer will ensure that the house of God is a place of purity, peace, prosperity, and power. We see this in 2 Chronicles 7:1 when, after Solomon finished praying, the fire of God fell in the house. This fire represented the presence of the Lord and everything named above.

The Lord promises in 2 Chronicles 7:14, "If my people, which are called by my name, shall humble themselves, and pray, and seek my face, and turn from their wicked ways; then will I hear from heaven, and will forgive their sin, and will heal their land." He goes on to say that His eyes and heart will forever be on this house as long as the people make prayer a top priority. Prayer is not to be secondary to anything in the house of the Lord. At a minimum, there should be a day or service set aside for nothing else but prayer.

In Luke 18:1, Jesus said, "Men ought to always pray, and not faint." Paul strongly exhorts, "Pray at all times (on every occasion, in every situation) in the Spirit, with all manner of prayer and entreaty; to that end keep alert and watch with strong purpose and perseverance, interceding in behalf of all the saints" (Ephesians 6:18 AMPC). "The earnest (heartfelt, continued) prayer of a righteous man makes tremendous power available" (James 5:16 AMPC). In short, no prayer, no power; little prayer, little power; much prayer, much power!

"...upon this rock I will build my church; and the gates of hell shall not prevail against it."

MATTHEW 16:18

The Pattern of the House 2

"Thou son of man, shew the house to the house of Israel, that they may be ashamed of their iniquities; and let them measure the pattern."

Ezekiel 43:10

The word *pattern* in Ezekiel, Chapter 43, means "the sum." The *Amplified Bible, Classic Edition,* says, "and let them measure accurately its appearance and plan." Another way of looking at it is to calculate (get the sum) the dimensions or arrangements or how the building will look upon completion. Keep in mind that Ezekiel was in the Spirit as He wrote this. Therefore, we are dealing with this as a spiritual house.

Furthermore, many things done physically in the Old Testament were "types and shadows" of the New Testament for our spiritual application. First Peter 2:5 bears this out: "Ye also, as lively stones, are built up a spiritual house." Ephesians 2:19-22 says that we are "of the household of God; and are built upon the foundation of the apostles and prophets, Jesus Christ himself being the chief corner stone; In whom all the building fitly framed together grows unto an holy temple in the Lord: In whom ye also are built together for an habitation of God through the Spirit."

Thus, the spiritual pattern refers to the people, not the physical building per se. Remember, Jesus, when declaring that He is building His church, used the word *ekklesia*, which means "called out ones" (Matthew 16). He is not referring as much to the physical edifice as He is to the people. More specifically, I will now begin to deal with the arrangement of the leadership and the function of membership in the Lord's house from a biblical perspective.

The Pastor

"And I will give you pastors according to mine heart, which shall feed you with knowledge and understanding."
JEREMIAH 3:15

The word *pastor* in Greek is *poimen*, meaning "shepherd, leader, overseer, guide, and servant." Let me point out that the pastor is not "The Shepherd" as Jesus is called, but he or she is what we call the "under-shepherd" or the shepherd under The Shepherd. It is equally important to point out that the pastor is still one of the sheep but is considered the "lead sheep." Therefore, a pastor should take great pleasure in being a "servant-leader" of God's flock of sheep.

A Gift from God

Like the rest of the five-fold ministry, a pastor is a gift from God. This does not mean that the pastor is more special than the rest of the congregation, but what it does mean is that the pastor is a gift according to Ephesians 4:8 and 11: "Wherefore he saith, when he ascended up on high, he led captivity captive, and gave gifts unto men; And he gave some apostles; and some prophets, and some evangelists; and some pastors and teachers." In this text, the word *gift* is *doma,* carrying the connotation of a gift made and a gift given. In other words, God first makes this gift into a pastor before becoming or being given as a pastor.

Born to Pastor

Pastoring requires a two-fold process. First, a pastor is born with the calling upon his or her life according to Jeremiah 1:5, "Before I formed thee in the belly I knew thee; and before thou came forth out of the womb I sanctified thee, and I ordained thee a prophet unto the nations." Secondly, a pastor must be developed through training and observation until the time of separation, as determined by the Holy Ghost and under the spiritual authority of the five-fold ministry or the government of God. A great example of this is in Romans 1:1 when the Apostle Paul wrote, "Paul, a servant of Jesus Christ, called to be an apostle, separated unto the gospel of God." Although Paul was born with the calling of an apostle, he served for observation for several years until he was separated by the prophets and teachers, who prayed, laid their hands on him, and then released him into his apostleship under the direction of the Holy Spirit, which was depicted in Acts, Chapter 13.

Pastor's Duties

Although pastors work in concert with the rest of the five-fold ministry to "perfect the saints" and help them mature, they are primarily responsible for their assignment, the members of their congregation. Acts, Chapter 6, outlines the principal duties of the pastor, beginning with the first appointment of deacons to take care of the business of "serving tables" (Verse 2). The word *serve* here is the Greek word *diakonos*, from which we derive the word *deacon*. This level of service meets the daily and practical needs of the people. In a real sense, the deacon serves as a liaison on behalf of the pastor. In Verse 4, we find the reason for the deacons and the two basic duties of every pastor, "But we will give ourselves continually to prayer, and to do the ministry of the word."

Feed the Flock

The word *ministry* in Acts 6:4 is *diakonia*, which means "care" and "service." Pastors' service includes continual prayer to hear from the Shepherd the word that should be ministered to the people. To better understand this, let's look at the dialogue between Jesus and Peter in John, Chapter 21. Jesus asked Peter if he loved Him three times. After Peter responded yes each time, Jesus directed him to feed His lambs and sheep. I point this out because the word *pastor* is the Greek noun *poimen*, and the word *feed* is the verb form *poinmaino*. This means if you love Me, Peter, then go and pastor (*poimen*) as an under-shepherd." However, you can't just feed (*poimaino*) them anything unless you come to Me as the Shepherd so that I can tell you what to feed them.

This is why the Lord says in Jeremiah 3:15, "And I will give you pastors according to mine heart, which shall feed you with knowledge and understanding." Just like David, a pastor will always seek the heart of God in order to feed the members what the Shepherd wants them to have. Thus, pastors FEED. It acrostically stands for Food, Example, Exhortation, Development. For food, The pastor always brings spiritual food provided by the Shepherd. For example, the pastor serves as an example by practicing what he preaches. For exhortation, the pastor serves as an exhorter to encourage the flock of God not to give up. For development, the pastor serves as a developer to help the sheep grow up in the things of God.

The Pulpit

"And Ezra the scribe stood upon a pulpit of wood, which they had made for the purpose."
NEHEMIAH 8:4

The word *pulpit* appears once in the Scriptures. However, the Hebrew word for pulpit, *migdal,* is recorded several times. Migdal translates as *tower* or *rostrum.* In Habakkuk 2:1, the prophet proclaimed, "I will stand upon my watch, and set me upon the tower (*migdal*), and will watch to see what he will say unto me, and what I shall answer when I am reproved." The pulpit is used to declare what the Lord is saying to the people. It is the primary place where the preachers (five-fold ministers) do their work. The pulpit is a wooden t-bridge, a worktable or desk, and a watch tower. In a real sense, the "pull-pit" is used by the pastor to pull the people out of the pit.

A Wooden T-Bridge

The pulpit is usually made of wood and centered upon a readied platform. The wood signifies our connection with God through the cross of Jesus Christ. The raised platform causes the pastor and the people to look unto the Lord for deliverance, much like Jesus being crucified on a wooden cross and raised on Golgotha's hill for all mankind to look up and live. The centered wooden pulpit signifies Jesus Christ as the only mediator between God and man (1 Timothy 2:5). Much like the cross, the pulpit denotes a "t-bridge" between heaven and earth to connect us with the Almighty God. When we look at the pulpit and the cross, it reminds us that Jesus is the only "bridge over troubled waters."

A Worktable

The pulpit is often referred to as a worktable or sacred desk because it is where the pastor and the other five-gold ministry members work or preach. In Nehemiah 8:1, the people spoke unto Ezra to bring the book or to preach the Word of God. The people gathered themselves together to "hear with understanding" (Nehemiah 8:2), and Ezra stood upon the pulpit and began to preach. At this juncture, it is vitally important to point out that the pulpit is not to be confused with a podium. The pulpit's purpose is for preaching, and the podium's primary use is for public speaking.

Often, churches have the pulpit on the side instead of the middle, where it should be. When this happens, the pulpit is out of symmetry. Podiums, most often, are placed on the side because something else will be the focus on the stage, such as a fashion show, play, dancers etc. Quite often, more than one podium is set up for narrators and guest speakers. In contrast, the pulpit is always centered because the only focus is on Jesus Christ and what He will say to us. It also signifies that there is only one way to reach heaven, and it is through Him. The tower of Babel is an excellent example of people trying to reach God without His help (Genesis 11). Is it any wonder they were confounded and scattered, and their efforts were brought to no avail?

A Watch Tower

> *"I will stand upon my watch, and set me upon the tower (migdal), and will watch to see what he will say unto me, and what I shall answer when I am reproved."*
>
> HABAKKUK 2:1

The pulpit is also a tower, where the pastor and the people watch to hear what thus saith the Lord. For this reason, the pulpit should be approached prayerfully. A pastor does not have anything to say if he or she has not first heard from God in prayer. In prayer, the pastor receives the vision for God's people and then proceeds to preach the Word so that the people might also receive the vision. It is important to note that a vision cannot be taught but must be caught in the spirit of revelation. Therefore, the people must also prayerfully approach the pulpit (watch tower). When the pulpit is esteemed appropriately, it becomes as Proverbs 18:10 declares, "The name of the LORD is a strong tower: the righteous run into it, and is safe."

All in all, if the house belongs to the Lord, there should be a pastor, under-shepherd, and servant-leader assigned to feed and nurture the people from the pulpit: "For the perfecting, equipping, and maturing of the saints, that they should do the work of ministering toward building up Christ's body (the church)" (Ephesians 4:12 AMPC).

The First Lady

"The elder unto the elect lady and her children, whom I love in the truth; and not only I, but also all they that have known the truth."

2 JOHN 1

Right from the start, let me say that I am not implying or trying to establish the first lady as an office of leadership in the church. Still, I am purposely magnifying her significance in the Lord's house and her value to the members that her husband pastures. The shame of the average church is that the first lady is a second-rate citizen, or at best, just a pretty face on the second row; some denominations will not even allow her to sit in the first row! To make matters worse, many first ladies are not even viewed as spiritual and are, therefore, hindered from functioning alongside their husbands to help him perfect the members. I am not saying that every first lady will preach from the pulpit or even that she will lead the women's group. My sincerest intention is to show from scripture that the first lady is an appropriate designation that should be acknowledged, received, and respected similarly to the pastor.

A Chosen Vessel

To see this, it is necessary that I first define three words: elect, first, and first lady. According to the *Vine's Expository Dictionary of New Testament Words*, the Greek word for *elect* is *eklektos*, which means "picked out, chosen/selected; chosen to be of especially high rank in administrative association with God; and a vessel of choice for a special purpose." The *Random House College Dictionary* defines *first* as "before all others with respect to time, order, rank, and importance" and *first lady* as "the foremost woman in any part, profession or the like," In sum, the elect or first lady is the foremost woman, before all other women in the church, a chosen vessel of especially high rank for a special purpose. First Peter 1:2 says that we are "elect according to the foreknowledge of God," which means before she was in the womb, God knew that she would marry a pastor and be known as the first lady.

A Spiritual Mother

Most saints will agree that a true pastor is called from the womb, according to Jeremiah 1:5. Therefore, we must also agree that God knew who his wife would be! Furthermore, most will agree that a pastor is a spiritual father. What does that make the pastor's wife, except a spiritual mother? I want you to get that the first lady is to be a spiritual mother, mentor, model, motivator, and minister in whatever way she is gifted by grace to function. When I say grace, I am talking about her motivational or creational gift, according to Romans 12, and the power and equipment provided by the Holy Spirit.

The Preacher's Wife

Genesis 20 records a fascinating story that illustrates the spiritual significance of the first lady. Abraham and Sarah had journeyed south and ran into the king of Gerar, Abimelech. Abraham introduced Sarah to the king as his sister out of fear that the king would kill him and take her anyway. Before the king could come near her, the Lord spoke to him in a dream, saying, "Behold, thou are but a dead man, for the woman which thou hast taken; for she is man's wife" (Genesis 20:43). Abimelech's response to the Lord was that he was innocent because Abraham affirmed that she was his sister. The Lord said to the king, "Now therefore restore the man his wife; for he is a prophet, and he shall pray for thee, and thou shalt live: and if thou restore her not, know thou that thou shalt die, thou, and all that are thine" (Genesis 20:7).

Abimelech quickly restored Abraham and his wife, granted him favor in the land, and blessed him with a thousand pieces of silver. I submit to you that this display of kindness and favor was not just because of the warning but because of the prophet's wife. I predicate this assertion upon Verses 17-18, where Abraham prayed for the king, his wife, children and servants: "For the Lord had fast closed up all wombs of the house of Abimelech, because of Sarah Abraham's wife." The Lord had shut this kingdom down, not because of the prophet, but because of the prophet's wife. Proverbs 18:22 outlines this kind of favor: "Whoso findeth wife findeth a good thing, and obtaineth favour of the LORD." The favor of the LORD comes not just from the preacher but from the preacher's wife.

The Foremost Woman

I am not saying, I repeat, I am not saying that every first lady will serve as a part of leadership, preach from the pulpit, or do anything that she does not possess the anointing or a calling to do. I am saying that she is a vessel of choice; she is to be highly honored, respected and regarded, and she should be highly spiritual. First lady is an appropriate designation for the foremost woman in the church, just as in the White House or any other organization.

The Elders

"And when they had ordained them elders in every church, and had prayed with fasting, they commended them to the Lord, on whom they believed."

ACTS 14:23

An elder, by definition, is someone older, eldest, senior, or advanced in life. When someone is considered an elder, it is assumed or expected that he or she is mature and possesses some level of life experience. The Bible refers to three different types of elders: Jewish, Gentile, and Church Elders. Thus, it is important to differentiate between them. First, Jewish Elders provided leadership as heads of tribes or families. Secondly, Gentile (non-Jewish) Elders held high rank and positions of authority. Lastly, we have Christian Church Elders, which will be addressed in more detail.

Elders are Essential

In Acts 14, the apostles or pastors ordained elders in every church. This divine process dates back to the early Old Testament times. We first read about the appointment of elders in Exodus 18, when Moses' father-in-law, Jethro, visited him in the wilderness. During this visit, Jethro observed that Moses, a type of pastor, sat to judge the people from morning until evening. Jethro, whose name means excellent, begins to counsel Moses concerning "a more excellent way." He basically told Moses that he would destroy himself if he did not get some people to assist him with his congregation of roughly several million people.

Elders Selected

Exodus 18:21-22 captures the main thrust of Jethro's counsel: "Moreover thou shalt provide out of all the people able men (elders), such as fear God, men of truth, hating covetousness; and place such over them, to be rulers of thousands, and rulers of hundreds, rulers of fifties, and rulers of tens; And let them judge the people at all seasons: and it shall be that every great matter they shall bring unto thee, but every small matter they shall judge: so shall it be easier for thyself, and they shall bear the burden with thee." During this counseling session, Jethro basically outlined the purpose and prerequisites for the approval and appointment of elders of the Lord's house.

Elder's Purpose

The overarching purpose of the elders was to serve with Moses as rulers or government of the people. They provided oversight of the congregation, assisted Moses in counseling and praying for the people, and ensured peace and victory for them. Another way of looking at this is the account found in Exodus 17 when Aaron and Hur (elders) held up the arms of Moses (pastor) while Joshua and the people were fighting the Amalekites. As long as the elders held Moses' hands up, the people (congregation) prevailed in the fight against the enemy, but when his arms dropped, the enemy prevailed. Holding up their arms, the elders support and assist the pastors where oversight is concerned.

Elders Today

Today, elders are appointed in the church pretty much the same way. The word *ordained* in Acts 14 carries the connotation of being prepared, approved, and then appointed. It means they receive orders of authorization to perform their duties and responsibilities as elders. These elders must meet the prerequisites in 1 Timothy 3 and Titus 1 and be competent, mature, and well-trained.

Elders hold up the arms of the pastor by assisting in government, overseeing the functions and services of the house, training the auxiliaries, praying for the people, preaching and teaching the Word of God, and providing counseling as needed. Numbers 11:16 says, "And the Lord said unto Moses, gather unto me seventy men of the elders…that they may stand there with thee." Then, in Verse 17, He says, "And I will come down and talk with thee there: and I will take the spirit which is upon thee and will put it upon them."

Faithful Elders

Elders should also possess the same spirit as the pastor, which should be displayed in their faithfulness to prayer, church attendance, tithing, love toward the people, and speaking the same thing. First Corinthians 1:10 bears this out, "Now I beseech you, brethren, by the name of our Lord Jesus Christ, that ye all speak the same thing, and that there be no divisions among you; but that ye be perfectly joined together in the same mind and in the same judgment."

In a nutshell, Christian Church Elders are ultimately those raised up and qualified by the Holy Spirit. Then, the pastor appoints them to have spiritual care and oversight of the congregation. Thus, elders must be ordained in every church if it is to be considered the Lord's house.

The Deacons

"Paul and Timothy, the servants of Jesus Christ, to all the saints in Christ Jesus which are at Philippi, with the bishops and deacons."

PHILIPPIANS 1:1

The first mention of the deacon can be traced back to the rapid growth of the early church. The deacon's ministry was birthed because the people multiplied so fast that the Apostles could not sufficiently meet all of their needs. Consequently, neglect set in, and the requirement for deacons became of utmost importance.

We pick up the narrative in Acts 6:1, "And in those days, when the number of the disciples was multiplied, there arose a murmuring of the Grecians against the Hebrews, because their widows were neglected in the daily ministration." We find in this text that the people had begun to murmur and complain because they were being neglected. In Verse 2, we see what the elders decided to do: "Then the twelve called the multitude of the disciples unto them, and said, it is not reason that we should leave the word of God and serve tables." They continued in Verses 3 and 4, "Wherefore, brethren, look ye out among you seven men of honest report, full of the Holy Ghost and wisdom, whom we may appoint over this business. But we will give ourselves continually to prayer, and to the ministry of the word."

Deacon Chosen

First of all, the elders considered the concept of serving tables as an important church business, which had to be done, but they also recognized that their primary job was to pray and feed the people the Word of God. Therefore, by the leading of the Holy Spirit, they decided to set aside qualified and anointed men to accomplish both missions simultaneously.

Secondly, the word *serve* in Verse 2 is the Greek word *diakonos*, where we get the English word *deacon*. According to the *Vine's Expository Dictionary*, *diakonos* or *deacon* primarily denotes a *servant*. It carries the connotation of an attendant, waiter, or one that provides relief. Generally speaking, a deacon is distinguished from a bondservant or slave in that it is more like a hired or household servant or one whose service is of freedom and dignity.

Dignified Servants

Simply put, a deacon is hired by and serves the Lord to serve the members of the Lord's house willingly and with utmost dignity. Is it any wonder that Verse 5 reveals that the appointment of deacons pleased the entire congregation and, therefore, the elders established the first seven deacons. Please note that deacons don't arbitrarily replace the pastor. They represent the pastor by ministering directly to the families, widows, and singles, thereby meeting their daily and practical needs. For example, when the deacons perform such duties as contacting the members, hospital visitations, and other menial tasks, it is as if the pastors do it themselves.

Deacon Qualifications

Let me point out that deacons must be chosen prayerfully and with much observation. In Acts 6, the deacons were full of the Holy Ghost, faith, and wisdom. They also had to meet the requisite qualifications found in 1 Timothy 3:1-13. Deacons must be investigated, proven, and prepared to function in this vitally important office.

The impact on the church when deacons are in place, is immeasurable: "And the word of God increased: and the number of the disciples multiplied in Jerusalem greatly; and a great company of the priests were obedient to the faith" (Acts 6:7). When deacons are appointed and function according to the word, the congregation will grow in stature, sum, and substance.

The Members

"But now has God set the members every one of them in the body, as it hath pleased him."
1 CORINTHIANS 12:18

> *"For as the body is one and hath many members, and all the members of that one body, being many, are one body: so also is Christ. For by one Spirit are we all baptized into one body...."*
>
> 1 Corinthians 12:12-13

When we receive Jesus as our personal savior, we immediately become members of the body of Christ. However, once we become members of the body, we need to become members of a local body of believers or what we call a local church assembly.

A Specific Assignment

This is much like when I joined the military. The day I raised my right hand and got sworn in, I became a member of the U.S. Army. Once I completed the required basic combat training and the advanced individual training to determine my specific job, I immediately received an assignment to Anbach, Germany, as a member of the First Armored Division, where I got assigned to a specific Kaserne (post) called Hindenburg, Kaserne. If that wasn't enough, I was finally assigned to a specific unit. All the while, no one asked me where I would like to work or be assigned, but I was told that everyone, without exception, was assigned to a unit.

Set by the Holy Spirit

Basically, over the 20-plus years that I served in the military, I was always a member of a specific unit, and I did not meet one soldier allowed to function as a "Rambo" or "Lone Ranger," going it alone or moving from unit to unit at will. The body of Christ works much the same way. Once we are born into the family of God, the Holy Spirit leads us to a local church where we can be fed, learn and grow. First Corinthians 12:18 makes this very clear: "But now hath God set the members every one of them in the body, as it pleased him."

No Exceptions!

According to 1 Corinthians 12:13, we are all born into and become members by the Holy Spirit. Then, the members are set in a body of believers, church, or local assembly. Let me also point out that the term "everyone" is used, which means this pertains to every single member and absolutely no one is excluded! Finally, it does not say, "as it pleased them," but as it pleased Him (God). I compare this to being born into this world. There is not one single person who had the privilege or opportunity to pick their mother, father, or even family for that matter.

Membership is God's idea. The Bible says, "Before I formed thee in the belly, I knew thee" (Jeremiah 1:5). Before you were conceived in the womb, the Lord decided the family He would set or assign you to. It is also much like the twelve tribes of Israel. They were born into the tribes and were not allowed to move from tribe to tribe at will or whim. I am trying to say that membership in the house of the Lord is and has always been God's idea. It is not an option! I cannot emphasize enough that this is not something for some and not for others. Every member born into the body of Christ must also be set as a member of a local church body wherever they are assigned.

The Bible says, "The steps of a good man are ordered by the Lord: and he delights in his way" (Psalm 37:23), which means every place you find yourself, as a child of God, is an assignment from the Lord, and he will lead you to the church where he will feed you. Church hopping is a very common occurrence throughout the body of Christ; I am convinced that it is why we have an "epidemic" of sorts where underdevelopment is concerned.

The average member who responds for deliverance, week after week, does not need deliverance but is in dire need of development. Many people will not sit still long enough to get some roots of the Word of God in them to grow up. Psalm 92:13 says, "Those that be planted in the house of the Lord shall flourish in the courts of our God." Like a rose, as long as it is planted and cared for, it will flourish, but if you pluck it up, it begins to die immediately!

Assembly Required!

Some may disagree with me and assert that it really does not make a difference as long as a person attends church. I submit that there is a vast difference between gathering at church and being assembled as a member. Permit me to provide the following to illustrate my point: Suppose you purchase a bicycle that requires assembly. The first thing you do is dump all of the parts from the box to inventory the contents. Your examination reveals all the parts are present. In case you don't know, the instruction manual says, "assembly required" before usage. Now, no matter how badly you want to ride your bike, you cannot ride a bike that has not been assembled, even though all the parts are present and there are no deficiencies.

Assembled Correctly

The following illustration will further magnify this point. Let's say that in the same way you purchase a child's swing-set for little John-John. This time, you are in the process of assembling it so that John-John can enjoy it. A review of the manual reveals detailed instructions that seem difficult to follow. You decide that the picture is sufficient enough to get the job done. Upon completion, the swing set looks exactly like the picture, but you have a few nuts and bolts left over that appear to be "extra." John-John is so excited to see the swing set and gets right in one of the swings. The problem is that the swing will not swing, and John-John is having no fun! My point is that the Lord never meant for the members to simply gather together at church because we must be assembled correctly for the church to function according to its intended purpose.

The General Assembly

In Hebrews 12:22-23, we are called "the general assembly and church of the firstborn." In Hebrews 10:25, we are directed: "Not forsaking the assembling of ourselves together, as the manner of some is; but exhorting one another: and so much the more, as ye see the day approaching." A close examination of Ephesians 4:16 reveals the overall blessing of the church that is assembled: "From whom the whole body fit lay joined together and compacted by that which every joint supplies, according to the effectual working in the measure of every part, maketh increase of the body unto the edifying of itself in love." The concept of being fitly or perfectly joined indicates that we are "connected." Compacted shows our "commitment." Every joint or member supplies delineates we are "contributing," making increase in the body or "causing" the body to grow.

Assemble Yourselves

It is made evident by the text that members assembled together are "better together," "teamwork makes our dreams work," and "together each achieves more." So now, every member of the body of Christ, hear the Word of the Lord according to Jeremiah 4:5-6, "Declare ye in Judah, and publish in Jerusalem; and say, Blow ye the trumpet in the land: cry, gather together, and say, Assemble yourselves, and let us go into the defenced cities. Set up the standard toward Zion (church): retire, stay not: for I will bring evil from the north, and a great destruction." The Lord is assembling us together as an exceeding great army, and the local church is a unit of assignment. What unit are you in, soldier of the living God?

The Helps Ministry

> *"And God hath set some in the church, first apostles, secondarily prophets, thirdly teachers, after that miracles, then gifts of healings, helps, governments, diversities of tongues."*
>
> 1 CORINTHIANS 12:28

The Helps Ministry is one of the most, if not the most, understaffed ministries in many churches. The statistics are downright appalling, reporting that, in the average church, 20% of the members do all the serving and giving, while the other 80% do nothing at all. Someone once said, "So many people just sit, soak, and sour," contributing nothing to the function of the Lord's house. An amusing way to look at this is what has been referred to as the "Tator Family," which includes Aggie Tator (agitator), Common Tator (commentator), Dick Tator (dictator), Hezzi Tator (hesitator), Imma Tator (imitator), and Spect Tator (spectator). Despite these, thanks be to God, one member, Participa Tator (participator), puts his hands to the plow and does not look back (Luke 9:62).

No Help at All

In the letter to the saints at Thessalonica, Paul advised, "For even when we were with you, this we commanded you, that if any would not work, neither should he eat" (2 Corinthians 3:10). In Verse 11, Paul even reveals the result of having non-working members, "For we hear that there are some which walk among you disorderly, working not at all, but are busybodies." Is it any wonder that some churches are in such disarray and busybodies are prevalent? Further, Paul, speaking by the Spirit, exhorted the saints, saying, "Now them that are such we command and exhort by our Lord Jesus Christ, that with quietness they work, and eat their own bread" (2 Thessalonians 3:12).

Obedience Required

Finally, in Verses 13 through 15, we get some really strong words concerning this unproductive behavior, as Paul admonished, "But ye, brethren, be not weary in well doing. And if any man obey not our word by this epistle, note that man, and have no company with him, that he may be ashamed. Yet count him not as an enemy, but admonish him as a brother." While these are very strong words, they convey the heart of the Lord, where the duties, functions, and maintenance of His house are concerned.

No More Excuses

Some of the most common responses to the cry for help in the church are "I don't know what to do," "The Lord has not revealed to me what to do; therefore, I am still praying," or better yet, "This church is so large, everything seems to be covered." The biblical answer to these and other excuses is found in Ecclesiastes 9:10, "Whatsoever thy hand finds to do, do it with thy might." I have been taught that the effective range of an excuse is zero! There is always work to be done in the local church where you are connected as a member. While praying and expecting an answer from the Lord, put your hands to something. For instance, there are never enough people to keep the church facilities clean inside and out.

Assembled for Effectiveness

As previously stated, the members of the house must not only be assembled but also assembled correctly. In the swing set illustration, John-John found out the hard way that he could not swing in a swing set assembled improperly. Imagine a bicycle assembled with the seat placed where the handlebars should be or the chain used for one of the tires. I think you get the point. So, it is with the church that unless assembled correctly and all members function appropriately, it will not operate as the Lord intended. Therefore, we become ineffective in reaching our city, nation, and the world. I am not implying that you should immediately begin working upon joining the church because this would be improper in most cases. I am simply emphasizing the significance of the proper assembly of the church to function effectively.

Having Enough Loving People Serving (HELPS)

The Bible clearly delineates what we should do to become productive members of a local church, and I will now explore this in more detail. However, before going any further, let's define this word *helps*. The Greek word is *antilepsis*, which is a compound word from *anti* and *lepsis*. *Anti* means "opposite to" and "from." *Lepsis* means "to support" or "to assist." We can accomplish the task if we have someone opposite to and from to support or assist. For example, if you need to move a table that requires at least two people, you can only move it if someone is opposite to and from you to support or assist.

This word *helps* connotes participating, being a partner and ultimately being a partaker. Note that the root word *part* is a key element in the concept of helps (remember this, as it will come in handy as we move along). Lastly, this word *helps* carries the connotation "to hold together in tough times." A church with a strong Helps Ministry better weathers the storms that come to destroy it and its members. The acrostic format for H.E.L.P.S. gives an easy understanding: Having Enough Loving People Serving.

Choose the Good Part

"In the beginning was the Word, and the Word was with God, and the Word was God."

JOHN 1:1

We should always start with the Word by giving the Word first place in every situation, especially where church membership is concerned. What I mean by this is we, like Mary, must choose the good part, the Word of God.

Luke 10:38-42 says, "Now it came to pass, as they went, that he entered into a certain village: and a certain woman named Martha received him into her house. And she had a sister called Mary, which also sat at Jesus' feet, and heard his word. But Martha was cumbered about with much serving, and came to him, and said, Lord, dost thou not care that my sister hath left me to serve alone? bid her therefore that she help me. And Jesus answered and said unto her, Martha, Martha, thou art careful and troubled about many things: But one thing is needful: and Mary hath chosen that good part, which shall not be taken away from her."

Many people, like Martha, are "busy as beavers" in the house of the Lord. Now, the Lord did not necessarily rebuke Martha for serving; He showed the priority of putting the Word first. I am trying to say that the only thing needed first is to choose the good part: to sit down and hear the Word. Notice, I did not say to check to see if the choir is good or if there is a good children's program, not that I am diminishing the importance of these things. However, we must place a greater value on the Word of God because "Faith comes by hearing, and hearing by the word of God" (Romans 10:17).

We are admonished in Ecclesiastes 5:1, "Keep thy foot when thou go to the house of God, and be more ready to hear, than to give the sacrifice of fools." We must place a higher premium upon hearing the Word when we come to church, above working in the church, because our very lives depend upon our ability to hear the Word of God. Jesus went to great lengths to teach the significance of the Word sown into good ground and even declared that hearing is the way of the kingdom. He calls the Word of God the good seed and the Word of the kingdom.

Imparting Your Part

In Matthew 1:23, Jesus says, "But he that received seed into the good ground is he that hears the word, and understands it, which also bears fruit, and brings forth, some an hundredfold, some sixty, some thirty." So when you choose the good part, the Lord imparts your part! Paul states, "For it is God which works in you both to will and to do of his good pleasure" (Philippians 2:1). The *Amplified Bible, Classic Edition,* expresses this text: "[Not in your own strength] for it is God Who is all the while effectually at work in you [energizing and creating in you the power and desire]...." The Holy Spirit gives life to the Word, produces a desire or unction to function, and empowers you to do your part by faith. Otherwise, you will be as James 2:20 says, "But wilt thou know, O vain man, that faith without works is dead?" The word *dead* here means "lifeless, inactive, ineffective, and worthless." So, it is with members who never get around to doing their part.

Do Your Part

Let's look at the concept of "your part" in light of Galatians 6. In Verse 2, Paul says, "Bear ye one another's burdens, and so fulfill the law of Christ." The word *burdens* is *baros*, which means "heavy" or "burdensome." In Verses 4 and 5, Paul continues, "But let every man prove his own work, and then shall he have rejoicing in himself alone, and not in another. For every man shall bear his own burden." This word *burden* is *phortion*, which means "easy" or "light." The inference is the member that bears his own burden (*phortion*) carries a light load. Jesus said, "Come unto me, all ye that labour and are heavy laden, and I will give you rest. For my yoke is easy, and my burden is light" (Matthew 11:29). However, when a member does not bear his own burden (*phortion*), someone has to bear several burdens (*baros*), which become heavy, burdensome or just too much to bear. Therefore, members experience burnout in the church, causing some to become overworked and leave altogether.

Now Take Part

Another implication concerning members who do not do their part is they often complain that they don't feel like they are a part of the family and ultimately leave the church. Members who begin to do their part will inevitably feel like they are a part of the church family. The active member will start to refer to the house as "my church," "my pastor," and "my brothers and sisters." This productive member then begins to take part or partake in the blessings and benefits of being a member of that local body of believers. "Giving thanks unto the Father, which has made us meet to be partakers of the inheritance of the saints in light…" (Colossians 1:12).

Laborers in the Church

In the parable of the laborers in the vineyard, Jesus paints a beautiful picture of the Lord's ownership and our partnership as it relates to being partakers of the benefit as we serve in the Lord's house. We find this marvelous illustration in the Book of Matthew, Chapter 20. It starts in Verse 1 by depicting the Father as the householder or owner, the members as the laborers, and, for the purpose of our study, the vineyard as the Lord's house. In Verse 2, the owner establishes wages for all laborers to be the same for a day's work. In Verses 3 through 7, the owner finds people standing by idly and hires them to work in his vineyard. Note that this was done at the third hour, ninth hour, and again at the eleventh hour, which means the workers started at different times throughout the day.

The Same Wages

In Verses 8 through 10, we find the workday over and the laborers receiving their day's wages. Each worker received their agreed-upon wages. Even though some started the third hour while others began at later hours, they got the same wage. Verse 11 reveals that those who had worked the longest, and possibly the hardest, started to complain against the owner of the house, "Saying, these have wrought but one hour, and thou hast made them equal unto us, which have borne the burden and heat of the day" (Verse 12). The owner's reply in Verse 13 flows from a righteous heart. He said, "Friend, I do thee no wrong: didst not thou agree with me for a penny?"

The Righteous Owner

He finishes the parable by declaring that as the owner, he could lawfully do as He desired and that the last would be paid just as the first. I love this parable because it reveals how we, as members of the house of the Lord, are afforded promises and benefits no matter when we start work or what specific job we do. There are no big "I's" or little "You's" when it comes to the Lord, the Master and Owner of the house, and all of the members. Paul says in Romans 2:10-11, "But glory, honour, and peace, to every man that worketh good, to the Jew first, and also to the Gentile: For there is no respect of persons with God." Like the laborers in this parable, every member is an equal partaker of the promised wages and the blessings of serving our Master and Owner, Jesus Christ!

---

*"God's plan is always
more beautiful than our desire."*

UNKNOWN

SHOW THE HOUSE TO THE HOUSE

The Form of the House 3

"And if they be ashamed of all that they have done, shew them the form of the house, and the fashion thereof, and the goings out thereof, and the comings in thereof, and all the forms thereof, and all the ordinances thereof, and all the forms thereof, and all the laws thereof: and write it in their sight, that they may keep the whole form thereof, and all the ordinances thereof, and do them."

Ezekiel 43:11 (KJV)

The word *form* in Ezekiel 43:11 is the Hebrew word *tsuwrah* (pronounced *tsura*), and it is the same as the Greek equivalent *petra*. Jesus used the word *petra* in Matthew 16:18 when He said, "…upon this rock (*petra*) I will build my church; and the gates of hell shall not prevail against it." The point is that the concept of the form of the house in this text bespeaks of the foundation. Most would agree that a strong foundation is the most critical aspect of constructing a building. A building erected upon a faulty foundation will eventually lean, produce cracked walls, and, what's worse, will come crashing down over time.

The Foundation

The house of the Lord is no different than any other building. Psalm 11:3 bears this out: "If the foundations be destroyed, what can the righteous do?" It is absolutely critical that we get the foundation right, or the rest of the building will not stand. Again, we are discussing the spiritual house of God or the people of God; therefore, the foundation refers to the fundamental principles of the Word of God. Hebrews 5:12 refers to this as "the first principles of the oracles of God." First Peter 1:2 says, "As newborn babes desire the sincere milk of the word, that ye may grow thereby," emphasizing building big, strong, and healthy people and not necessarily on a big, physical edifice. Of course, strong and healthy members will ultimately result in church growth as well.

Basic Fundamentals

One word that captures the concept of foundation or fundamental principles is doctrine. Doctrine simply means teaching. It carries the connotation of teaching the first principles or "the basics." In a nutshell, doctrine is the preaching and teaching of fundamental principles that establish your belief system and the foundation for your faith. In other words, the first thing you should learn and know is what you believe; and it should be the Bible plus nothing else! There are two basic categories of doctrine: sound and strange. Permit me to address them now.

Sound Doctrine

Paul, writing to young pastor Timothy, gave him the following charge in 2 Timothy 4:1-4, "I charge thee therefore before God, and the Lord Jesus Christ, who shall judge the quick and the dead at his appearing and his kingdom; Preach the word; be instant in season, out of season; reprove, rebuke, exhort with all longsuffering and doctrine. For the time will come when they will not endure sound doctrine; but after their own lusts shall they heap to themselves teachers, having itching ears; And they shall turn away their ears from the truth, and shall be turned unto fables." The word *sound* here means "true, incorruptible, unadulterated, right, reliable, and healthy." It implies that which helps and causes you to grow. Note that, in this text, the word *sound* is singular because there is only one. This one sound doctrine in Hebrews 6:1-3 is called the doctrine of Christ, which we will discuss in more detail later.

No Other Doctrine

We must ensure our doctrine is right because it is the foundation for our faith, and there is grave danger in not making sure we have the one sound doctrine according to the Scriptures. The Apostle John admonishes us in 2 John 1:9-11, "Whosoever transgresseth, and abideth not in the doctrine of Christ, hath not God. He that abideth in the doctrine of Christ, he hath both the Father and the Son. If there come any unto you, and bring not this doctrine, receive him not into your house, neither bid him God speed: For he that biddeth him God speed is partaker of his evil deeds." The Apostle Paul takes it a little further in Romans 16:17-18, "Now I beseech you, brethren, mark them which cause divisions and offences contrary to the doctrine which ye have learned; and avoid them. For they that are such serve not our Lord Jesus Christ, but their own belly; and by good words and fair speeches deceive the hearts of the simple."

Paul calls it "the doctrine." It's a definite article and implies that we should have learned it to avoid those who come contrary to it. It is a sad state of affairs when the people of God are not growing, and consequently, the church won't grow. Chances are the doctrine is not sound or healthy. Thus, Paul writes in 1 Timothy 4:16, "Take heed unto thyself, and unto the doctrine; continue in them: for in doing this thou shalt both save thyself, and them that hear thee." We must pay attention to our doctrine and make sure it is sound, and we will be able to save ourselves and others, too!

Strange Doctrines

> *"Be not carried about with divers and strange doctrines. For it is a good thing that the heart be established with grace; not with meats, which have not profited them that have been occupied therein."*
>
> HEBREWS 13:9

Notice that strange doctrines in this text are plural. This means that there is more than one. I submit to you that there are at least four types of strange doctrines, and while I am not saying that there are no others, I will address these four at this time.

First, let's define the word *strange*, which means "false, foreign, unfamiliar, odd, and corrupt." It implies that which stunts your growth and ultimately leads to destruction. Strange doctrine is the direct opposite of that which is sound. Let me point out that I will not attempt to exhaust these strange doctrines, but I will endeavor to show the effects on the church where they exist and how to recognize them. The four strange doctrines I will address are embedded within the illustration of the seven churches of Asia Minor according to Revelations, Chapters 2 and 3.

1. The Doctrine of Balaam

The first strange doctrine is found in the church of Pergamos in Revelation 2:14, called the doctrine of Balaam. This refers to the prophet Balaam, who King Balak hired to curse the children of Israel. Long story short, Numbers 22:22 says, "And God's anger was kindled because he (Balaam) went." It upset God that Balaam would even consider doing this for money. Consequently, Balaam was a prophet for hire. The doctrine of Balaam represents democracy in the church. This doctrine is identified in churches where the people rule over the preacher by manipulation. The people exercise the "power of the vote" and, therefore, control the preacher, rendering them unable to follow the voice of God.

2. The Doctrine of the Nicolaitanes

In the same verse, the second strange doctrine is called the doctrine of the Nicolaitanes. Derived from the name *Nicholas*, it refers to the days when Nicholas ruled. The name Nicholas means dominator of the people. It is much like the pharaoh in the book of Exodus when it says he was a hard taskmaster. This doctrine represents autocracy in the church, and it is identified by the preacher overruling the people with domination. It is one thing to rule over the people with the Word of God, which also applies to the preacher, but God gives no man authority to overrule anyone. Peter writes, "Neither as being lords over God's heritage, but being an ensample to the flock" (1 Peter 5:3).

3. The Doctrine of Devils

The third strange doctrine is found in Revelations 2:20 in the church of Thyatira, and it is called the doctrine of devils. This church allowed a woman, with the spirit of Jezebel (seduction), to teach and seduce the people to sacrifice to idols. This doctrine represents idolatry in the church. Demons of deception and seduction rule the people and their preacher with the idols of money to man and his gifting. Paul warns Pastor Timothy "that in the latter times some shall depart from the faith, giving heed to seducing spirits, and doctrines of devils" (1 Timothy 4:1).

4. The Doctrine of Men

In Revelations 3, the fourth and final strange doctrine comes from the church of Sardis. The scripture says of this church that they have a name or reputation, but they are dead. In other words, they had a form of godliness but denied its power (2 Timothy 3:5). This is what is known as the doctrine of men and represents hypocrisy in the church. The churches with this doctrine can be identified by strict adherence to tradition and strong condemnation. The Bible says that the Word of God is made of no effect because of the tradition of men (Mark 7:13).

It's Time to Grow Up

Ephesus 4:14 challenges us, "That we henceforth be no more children, tossed to and fro, and carried about with every wind of doctrine, by the sleight of men, and cunning craftiness, whereby they lie in wait to deceive; But speaking the truth in love, may grow up into him in all things, which is the head, even Christ." All of these and other strange doctrines are a part of Satan's plan to deceive the people of God and cause them to be led away from Jesus Christ. We must recognize and avoid them by staying rooted and grounded in a good church where sound doctrine is the only foundation, which ultimately results in us growing up.

The Doctrine of Christ

Although many church, denominational or religious doctrines exist, only one doctrine, scripturally speaking, has been identified as sound: the Doctrine of Christ. The Lord's house (people of God) is to be built on a sure foundation. First Corinthians 3:11 tells us, "For other foundation can no man lay than that is laid, which is Jesus Christ." Jesus is the only authorized foundation on which the Lord will allow His house to be built without exception. He is the Rock, in Matthew 7, that the wise man built on, and the storms could not destroy his house. The church built upon the doctrine of Christ will inevitably grow and be strong enough to withstand the onslaught of the wicked one.

This doctrine is found in Hebrews 6:1-3, stating, "Therefore leaving the principles of the doctrine of Christ, let us go on unto perfection; not laying again the foundation of repentance from dead works, and of faith toward God, Of the doctrine of baptisms, and of laying on of hands, and of resurrection of the dead, and of eternal judgment. And this will we do, if God permits." I will briefly address the six foundational stones or fundamental teaching of the doctrine of Christ.

1. Repentance From Dead Works

The word *repentance* is a kingdom concept rarely mentioned in the world. In a real sense, repentance is the only way into the kingdom of God. John the Baptist preached the need to repent in Matthew 3:1, saying, "Repent ye, for the kingdom of heaven is at hand." At the beginning of Jesus' ministry, Matthew 4:17 records, "From that time Jesus began to preach, and to say, Repent: for the kingdom of heaven is at hand." And finally, under the influence of the Holy Spirit, the Apostles began their ministries preaching, "Repent, and be baptized every one of you in the name of Jesus Christ for the remission of sins…" (Acts 2:38).

The Prerequisite is Brokenness

Before delving into this concept of repentance, I must first address the prerequisite. Brokenness is the prerequisite to true repentance. Brokenness amounts to the Holy Spirit's conviction of your heart. It is where the Holy Spirit begins to influence you to submit your will to God's will. In Acts 2, after Peter preached his first message, the people asked, what must we do? Verse 37 says, "Now when they heard this, they were pricked in their heart, and said unto Peter and the rest of the apostles, Men and brethren, what shall we do?" They were so convicted in their hearts that they were ready to do whatever the Lord required. Recognizing their brokenness, Peter replied, "Repent" in Verse 38. Genuine brokenness causes one to cry out as David did in Psalm 51:3, "For I acknowledge my transgressions: and my sin is ever before me." When a man experiences brokenness, repentance will surely follow.

Turn from Dead Works

Now repent is the word *metanoia* in Greek, a compound word of *meta*, meaning "to change," and *noia*, meaning "the mind." It also connotes turning and going in a different direction. Biblical repentance means changing your mind by thinking, feeling, and doing differently. It is a 180-degree turn from the past life of sin to a new life in Jesus Christ. Repentance is not turning over a new leaf, as in New Year's resolution, because people turn from one bad thing to another. Repentance is to turn from an old life of sin to a new life of righteousness only found in Christ. When you repent, you are not only turning from your sins to God, but you are also repenting or turning from dead works.

Dead works are religious works that people do to try and earn favor with God. These works are the things we do to try and get God to accept us without confessing our sins. These works are very dangerous because they cause people to miss salvation altogether. Instead of facing God so that He can deal with our sins, we try to get Him to accept us as "not that bad." The truth is we are just not that good! The only thing that God will accept is true and honest repentance from dead works so that He can cleanse us from our sins.

2. Faith Toward God

The second principle in the doctrine of Christ is faith toward God. This principle is connected to and part of the first. When we repent and turn from dead works, we turn to "have faith in God" (Mark 11:22), where Jesus becomes the object and focus of our faith. Faith is a trust, confidence and belief that results in action. Believing becomes faith when you act upon it. Thus, the acrostic format reveals that F.A.I.T.H. is Forward Action in Trusting Him.

Now that Jesus is the object of our faith, we begin to understand that He does not just give us faith, but He is our faith. Our faith is not in something but in Someone; therefore, we will never have a faith failure because He will never fail us. That brings us to the objective of our faith, the Word of God. John 1:1 says, "In the beginning was the Word, and the Word was with God, and the Word was God." If we say we have faith in God, then we must have faith in His Word because He and His Word are one and the same. This means that we are standing on specific scriptural promises when we say we have faith in or toward God.

Finally, if the object of our faith is Jesus Christ, and the objective of our faith is in His Word, then we will begin to walk in the obedience of our faith. According to James 2, "Faith without works is dead." Therefore, obedience to faith releases faith by speaking, giving, or doing something. The Lord expects us to now "walk by faith, and not by sight" (2 Corinthians 5:7) and ultimately live in faith toward God every day.

3. The Doctrine of Baptisms

There are at least seven scriptural baptisms recorded in the Bible. I will not attempt to get into an in-depth teaching concerning these, but I will provide a list with a basic description and scriptural reference of all seven. But first, let's define the word *baptize*. The Greek word *baptizo* means "to dip into, submerge, immerse or to bury completely." Although one can be baptized into water, the word itself does not mean water. The following is a list of the seven biblical baptisms:

1 | The Baptism of Moses

> *"Moreover, brethren, I would not that ye should be ignorant, how that all our fathers were under the cloud, and all passed through the sea; And were all baptized unto Moses in the cloud and in the sea...."*
>
> 1 CORINTHIANS 10:1-2 (KJV)

This baptism is an Old Testament type of New Testament salvation. They were saved after partaking in the Passover supper, of which the slain lamb represented Jesus. It was not the water that saved them, but their partaking of the Passover. The Red Sea served as a sign or symbol of their salvation. Remember, each household had to kill the lamb, place its blood over the doorposts and lentils, and eat all of the lamb. Jesus said in John 6:53, "Verily, verily, I say unto you, Except ye eat the flesh of the Son of man, and drink his blood, ye have no life in you." They could only pass through the Red Sea after receiving the lamb.

2 | The Baptism of Repentance for the Remission of Sins

> *"John did baptize in the wilderness and preach the baptism of repentance for the remission of sins."*
>
> MARK 1:4 (KJV)

John the Baptist's baptism prepared the hearts of the people to receive Jesus Christ as the Messiah. The primary focus was two-fold: repentance and confession of sins. Both were required before John would baptize anyone. John even said they had to display fruit to show they had repented before being baptized. John was preparing them because the same two things would be required to receive Jesus as Savior from their sins.

3 | The Baptism into His Body

> *"For by one Spirit are we all baptized into one body, whether we be Jews or Gentiles, whether we be bond or free; and have been all made to drink into one Spirit."*
>
> 1 CORINTHIANS 12:13 (KJV)

When you are convicted by the Holy Spirit to receive Jesus as your Savior, the Holy Spirit baptizes you into the Body of Christ. This baptism has nothing to do with water, but it is a result of accepting the invitation to be born into Christ's body. Galatians 3:27-28 says, "For as many of you as have been baptized into Christ have put on Christ. There is neither Jew nor Greek, there is neither bond nor free, there is neither male nor female: for ye are all one in Christ Jesus." Salvation is a baptism into the body of Christ.

4 | The Baptism into Water

> *"And he commanded the chariot to stand still: and they went down both into the water, both Philip and the eunuch; and he baptized him."*
>
> Acts 8:38 (KJV)

According to 1 Peter 3, baptism in water does not save us but is an answer to a good conscience toward God. Ephesians 2:8-9 says, "For by grace are ye saved through faith; and that not of yourselves: it is the gift of God: Not of works, lest any man should boast." Water baptism demonstrates outwardly and publicly what has happened inwardly and privately. Salvation is truly a private matter, but baptism allows you to publicly show that you identify with the death, burial, and resurrection of Jesus Christ. We don't get baptized to get saved, but we get baptized to show the world I am saved!

An excellent illustration is in the account of Paul and Silas ministering to the prison keeper in Acts 16. In Verse 30, the keeper asks, "Sirs, what must I do to be saved?" This was the perfect time for Paul to say, "You need to be baptized in water." However, Verse 31 reveals Paul's response, "And they said, Believe on the Lord Jesus Christ, and thou shalt be saved, and thy house." After preaching the word to him and his household, they baptized every one of them (see Verses 32-33).

5 | The Baptism with the Holy Ghost

> *"For John truly baptized with water, but ye shall be baptized with the Holy Ghost not many days hence."*
>
> ACTS 1:5 (KJV)

This baptism is an experience that is subsequent to salvation. Also known as "The promise of the Father" (Acts 1:4) and "the gift of the Holy Ghost" (Acts 2:38), this free gift is promised to every Christian believer. Matthew 3:11 reveals Jesus as the baptizer with the Holy Ghost: "I indeed baptize you with water unto repentance: but he that cometh after me is mightier than I, whose shoes I am not worthy to bear: he shall baptize you with the Holy Ghost, and with fire." The main purpose for this baptism is for the Christian believer to receive supernatural power from the Holy Ghost (Acts 1:8) with the initial sign (evidence) of speaking in other tongues (see Acts 2:1-4, 8:14-20, 10:44-46, and 19:1-7).

6 | The Baptism with Fire

> *"John answered, saying unto them all, I indeed baptize you with water; but one mightier than I cometh, the latchet of whose shoes I am not worthy to unloose: he shall baptize you with the Holy Ghost and with fire...."*
>
> LUKE 3:16 (KJV)

Notice first that the baptism with the Holy Ghost and the baptism with fire are not one and the same but are two separate baptisms. The word *fire* comes from the Greek word *pur*, which bespeaks of "the holiness of God." The purpose of this baptism is to purify and consume all of the ungodliness from the Christian's life: "For our God is a consuming fire" (Hebrews 12:29). This is to purge us from worldliness so that we live in God's holiness. The fire of God also represents the presence and the power of God. To truly dwell in His presence and experience His power, we must allow this baptism to rid us of ungodliness and worldliness.

7 | The Baptism into His Sufferings

> *"And they said unto him, We can. And Jesus said unto them, Ye shall indeed drink of the cup that I drink of; and with the baptism that I am baptized withal shall ye be baptized…."*
>
> Mark 10:39 (KJV)

In this text of scripture, Jesus was referring to His suffering, not just on the cross, but all of the things he had to go through. This is why He called it the "cup" that He had to drink from and that all His disciples would have to drink from the same cup of suffering. Speaking to them concerning His impending crucifixion, Jesus said, "These things I have spoken unto you that in me ye might have peace. In the world ye shall have tribulation: but be of good cheer; I have overcome the world" (John 16:33). Tribulation represents three times the trouble, or the suffering of temptations, tests, and trials. He encouraged them to be of good cheer, for they would be able to endure suffering because He overcame the world. First Peter 4:1-2 captures the essence: "Forasmuch then as Christ hath suffered for us in the flesh, arm yourselves likewise with the same mind: for he that hath suffered in the flesh hath ceased from sin; That he no longer should live the rest of his time in the flesh to the lusts of men, but to the will of God." Paul wrote in 2 Timothy 3:12, "Yea, and all that will live godly in Christ Jesus shall suffer persecution." The bottom line is every child of God must inevitably experience this baptism and be identified with the sufferings of Christ.

4. The Laying on of Hands

The fourth foundational stone of the doctrine of Christ is the principle of the laying on of hands. This principle begins with God placing His hand upon man to empower him for service. In ancient times, the king would lay his hand upon his subjects, empower them, and send them out to carry out the business of his kingdom. The kingdom of God is no different: As we humble ourselves under the hand of our King, He blesses, empowers, and releases us to do His will. Therefore, the laying on of hands is a symbol or sign that shows we believe in King Jesus' ability to perform mighty acts through the working of the Holy Ghost, by signs, wonders, and miracles, and through the laying on of hands.

In Mark 16:17-18, Jesus declares, "And these signs shall follow them that believe; In my name shall they cast out devils; they shall speak with new tongues; They shall take up serpents; and if they drink any deadly thing, it shall not hurt them; they shall lay hands on the sick, and they shall recover." Notice that the sign of the laying on of hands, and all the other signs, will follow the believer. Now, there are three main purposes for the laying of hands: confirmation, separation, and impartation.

1 | *Confirmation and Affirmation*

First of all, confirmation means to affirm, to express agreement, or to declare something to be true. It means to bear witness to a spiritual calling in someone's life. While any well-meaning believer can do this, please take heed to Paul's warning. He admonishes all of us in 1 Timothy 5:22 to "Lay hands suddenly on no man...." If you do, you can become a partaker of that person's sin if, in fact, they are in sin. When done prayerfully, any believer can bear witness to a call to the ministry in a person's life through the laying on of hands. Be advised that this does not amount to you calling or releasing them into a ministry. Remember that the release into ministry must come through the five-fold ministry, which represents the government of God.

2 / Ordination for Separation

In ordination for separation, a person is anointed, set apart, and released into ministry. This separation is only done after close observation, while the minister makes full proof of his or her calling and by the approval of God. Further, the ordination can only be performed by someone with a higher anointing or under the authority of the five-fold ministry or the presbytery. First Timothy 4:14 says, "Neglect not the gift that is in thee, which was given thee by prophecy, with the laying on of the hands of the presbytery."

An excellent illustration that bears this out is in the ministry of the Apostle Paul found in Romans 1:1, "Paul, a servant of Jesus Christ, called to be an apostle, separated unto the gospel of God...." Paul was born with the calling of an apostle, but he ministered as a teacher and preacher of the Word of God until his separation. After years of being under observation, we find Paul being separated in Acts 13. "Now there were in the church that was at Antioch certain prophets and teachers; as Barnabas, and Simeon that was called Niger, and Lucius of Cyrene, and Manaen, which had been brought up with Herod the tetrarch, and Saul. As they ministered to the Lord, and fasted, the Holy Ghost said, Separate me Barnabas and Saul for the work whereunto I have called them. And when they had fasted and prayed, and laid their hands on them, they sent them away" (Acts 13:1-3).

3 | Impartation of God's Power

The anointing for impartation imparts the power to heal the sick, cast out evil spirits, and assist people in receiving the Holy Ghost. Two signs follow all who believe: cast out devils and heal the sick (Mark 16). Luke 9:1 says, "Then he (Jesus) called his twelve disciples together, and gave them power and authority over all devils, and to cure diseases." In Matthew 10:7-8, Jesus gives the following command: "And as ye go, preach, saying, The kingdom of heaven is at hand. Heal the sick, cleanse the lepers, raise the dead, cast out devils: freely ye have received, freely give." Luke 13:11-13 says, "And, behold, there was a woman which had a spirit of infirmity eighteen years, and was bowed together, and could in no wise lift up herself. And when Jesus saw her, he called her to him, and said unto her, Woman, thou art loosed from thine infirmity. And he laid his hands on her: and immediately she was made straight, and glorified God."

Lastly, Acts 8:14-17 records, "Now when the apostles which were at Jerusalem heard that Samaria had received the word of God, they sent unto them Peter and John: Who, when they were come down, prayed for them, that they might receive the Holy Ghost: (For as yet he was fallen upon none of them: only they were baptized in the name of the Lord Jesus.) Then laid they their hands on them, and they received the Holy Ghost." Tremendous power is released through the laying on of hands, and all believers must learn, preach, and practice it.

5. The Resurrection of the Dead

The concept of resurrection of the dead is often misconstrued as being raised from the dead. Yet, a vast difference exists between a resurrection and a dead person being raised. Accordingly, the story in Luke 11 documents Lazarus being raised from the head and not resurrected. When one is raised from the dead, he will die again. At the resurrection, there is no more death because the person has entered into eternity.

Jesus is the Resurrection

In John 11:21-26, we pick up the dialogue between Martha and Jesus concerning the resurrection: "Then said Martha unto Jesus, Lord, if thou hadst been here, my brother had not died. But I know, that even now, whatsoever thou wilt ask of God, God will give it thee. Jesus saith unto her, Thy brother shall rise again. Martha saith unto him, I know that he shall rise again in the resurrection at the last day. Jesus said unto her, I am the resurrection, and the life: he that believeth in me, though he were dead, yet shall he live: And whosoever liveth and believeth in me shall never die. Believest thou this?" The resurrection really is not something but Someone, Jesus Christ! What's more, the concept of resurrection involves redemption, reconciliation and restoration, all provided through our Lord and Savior, Jesus Christ.

Resurrection of the Just and Unjust

The Scriptures record two distinct resurrections: the first and the second. Also known as the resurrection of life and the resurrection of damnation (John 5:29), Act 24:15 records, "And have hope toward God, which they themselves also allow, that there shall be a resurrection of the dead, both of the just and the unjust."

The First Resurrection

The first resurrection refers to the resurrection of the saved or those who died in Christ. Often termed the "rapture," it more accurately describes it in scripture as being "caught up." First Thessalonians 4:13-17 describes this glorious occasion, "But I would not have you to be ignorant, brethren, concerning them which are asleep, that ye sorrow not, even as others which have no hope. For if we believe that Jesus died and rose again, even so them also which sleep in Jesus will God bring with him.

For this we say unto you by the word of the Lord, that we which are alive and remain unto the coming of the Lord shall not prevent them which are asleep. For the Lord himself shall descend from heaven with a shout, with the voice of the archangel, and with the trump of God: and the dead in Christ shall rise first: Then we which are alive and remain shall be caught up together with them in the clouds, to meet the Lord in the air: and so shall we ever be with the Lord." Thus, this emphasizes that only those who die in Christ will experience the first resurrection.

Choose a Resurrection

Revelation 14:13 says, "And I heard a voice from heaven saying unto me, Write, Blessed are the dead which die in the Lord...." The bottom line is the decision to accept and remain in Christ must be made before death; only then can you be sure that you are a part of the first resurrection. If you die outside of Christ, you will have to wait until the second resurrection or the resurrection of damnation, and ultimately stand before the Great White Throne of Judgment and be condemned forever for your sins. I will cover this in more detail as a part of the Eternal Judgment.

The Judgment Seat of Christ

> *For we must all appear before the judgment seat of Christ;*
> *that everyone may receive the things done in his body,*
> *according to that he hath done, whether it be good or bad.*
>
> 2 Corinthians 5:10 (KJV)

The Greek word for *judgment* in this text is *bema*, which bespeaks the award ceremony during the Greek Olympic Games. The point is that this will be an occasion for rewards and not condemnation. Notice, we will all stand before this judgment seat, which will be part of the "Marriage Supper of the Lamb" (Revelations 19:1-10).

Unconfessed Sins and Rewards

There are two main reasons for the judgment seat of Christ: The Lord will deal with us about unconfessed sins, and the Lord will reward us for our works or labors of love. If we don't deal with our sins before the Lord returns, He will deal with them at the judgment seat. Notice what Paul writes in Romans 14:10 and 12, "10 But why dost thou judge thy brother? or why dost thou set at nought thy brother? for we shall all stand before the judgment seat of Christ. 12 So then every one of us shall give account of himself to God." The only sins that the Lord will forgive are the ones we confess. So, we will do it now or later. Hebrews 10:30 says, "The Lord shall judge his people."

Works Made Manifest

Concerning the rewards, Paul writes, "For other foundation can no man lay than that is laid, which is Jesus Christ. Now if any man build upon this foundation gold, silver, precious stones, wood, hay, stubble; Every man's work shall be made manifest: for the day shall declare it, because it shall be revealed by fire; and the fire shall try every man's work of what sort it is. If any man's work abide which he hath built thereupon, he shall receive a reward. If any man's work shall be burned, he shall suffer loss: but he himself shall be saved; yet so as by fire" (1 Corinthians 3:11-15).

God is just and will reward us according to what we have done in this life. Some will rejoice to hear, "Well done, my good and faithful servant" (Matthew 25:21), because they have served the Lord with all their hearts. Others will be ashamed because they got saved but invested nothing into the kingdom of God, and all that they will hear is, "Well!"

6. The Eternal Judgment

The sixth and final principle of the doctrine is eternal judgment. The word *eternal* denotes that which is *endless* or *everlasting*. It means "infinite" or "without end." The Greed word for *judgment* here is *krima*, which means "condemnation" or "damnation." Therefore, this final principle deals with the eternal damnation or the final judgment of God that will last forever. This judgment will be for those who died outside of Christ and who were not part of the first resurrection. These are the unsaved people who rejected Jesus Christ and ultimately are part of the second resurrection unto damnation.

Heaven or Hell

According to Scripture, those who die in Christ go to be with the Lord. Second Corinthians 5:8 says, "We are confident, I say, and willing rather to be absent from the body, and to be present with the Lord." This is where the dead in Christ remain until the rapture. However, those who reject Jesus Christ and die outside of Him go to a place called hell, a temporary holding place until the eternal judgment. Some people don't believe that hell really exists, but the Bible is clear that hell is a real place where the unsaved go when they die.

Hell is a Real Place

The story in Luke 16:19-31 sheds light upon the destination of the saved and unsaved upon death. In this account, a beggar named Lazarus died and went into a place called "Abraham's bosom," and a rich man died and went to a place called hell. Interestingly enough, the angels carried the beggar to Abraham's bosom while the rich man went immediately into flames and torment. Let me point out that when Jesus shared a parable, He did not use names. Thus, Lazarus and this rich man lived on the earth at one time. Also, notice what the rich man said in Verse 27, "I pray thee therefore, father, that thou would send him to my father's house, for I have five brethren; that he may testify unto them, lest they come into this place of torment." This was not a dream, but as the rich man stated, this was a real place of torment.

Hell is Jail

The unsaved people who reject Jesus Christ and find themselves in this place called hell will have to remain there until one thousand years after the first resurrection. According to Revelations 20:11-12, the eternal judgment will take place at the Great White Throne of

God: "And I saw a great white throne, and him that sat on it, from whose face the earth and the heavens fled away; and there was found no place for them. And I saw the dead, small and great stand before God; and the books were opened: and another book was opened, which is the book of life: and the dead (those outside of Christ) were judged out of those things which were written in the books according to their works."

The Record Books

Notice that the "books" were opened first. All the sins that every unsaved person has committed are recorded in these books. It continues in Verse 13, "And the sea gave up the dead which were in it; and death and hell delivered up the dead which were in them: and they were judged every man according to their works." Remember that I previously stated that hell was like jail or a temporary holding place. "And death and hell were cast into the lake of fire. This is the second death."

The Book of Life

And whosoever was not found written in the book of life was cast into the lake of fire. "Blessed and holy is he that hath part in the first resurrection: on such the second death hath no power, but they shall be priests of God and Christ, and shall reign with him a thousand years" (Revelations 20:6). It is not the Lord's will that any man should be eternally damned, but the only way to avoid it is to accept Jesus Christ and ensure you die in Him. Please choose Jesus before it is too late!

"It is not the beauty of a building you should look at; it's the construction of the foundation that will stand the test of time."
DAVID ALLEN COE

SHOW THE HOUSE TO THE HOUSE

The Fashion of the House

4

"And if they be ashamed of all that they have done, shew them the form of the house, and the fashion thereof...."

Ezekiel 43:11 (KJV)

The Hebrew word for *fashion* in the above text is *tekuwna* (pronounced *tekuna*), which means arrangement, disposition, preparation, and a structure or fixed place.

Firstly, the arrangement points toward organization or that which is organized in an orderly fashion. We called it a formation in the military, arranging us by rank and job. In formation, we received our orders and instructions before the workday. Arrangement also connotes a congregation assembled and functioning properly.

Secondly, disposition signifies the character or nature, which results in the quality of function. Our disposition is of the highest quality because we possess the Spirit of excellence.

Thirdly, preparation denotes that detailed planning takes place before the execution of the function. Of course, all preparation includes training to ensure obedience to orders. Military personnel refer to this as discipline.

Lastly, the structure or fixed place suggests that which is permanently set. So much so, that it is likened unto a law: a fixed principle that leaves no room for negotiation, discussion or debate. In a nutshell, the fashion points to the order, which is essential in the house of the Lord.

Order in the House!

"For He [Who is the source of their prophesying] is not a God of confusion and disorder but of peace and order. As [is the practice] in all the churches of the saints (God's people)...."
1 Corinthians 14:33 AMPC

Paul, writing to the church at Corinth, enlightens them by saying that confusion and disorder should not be in the church because God is the author of peace and order. Notice Paul says that order should be practiced in all of the churches! Paul later writes in Verse 40, "But all things should be done with regard to decency and propriety and in an orderly fashion" (*Amplified Bible, Classic Edition*).

According to the *Vine's Expository Dictionary of New Testament Words*, the word *order* means "an arranging, arrangement or to arrange; to set, to ordain or to place; due order or that which is proper, correct, or right; it means to straighten out or organize."

It further says that the military term order denotes a company or formation and means to charge and give/take orders. This is where the military got its rank and command structure.

Someone once asked me if I was trying to make the church look like the military. I replied, "No. The military got the concept of order from God!" Order expresses the Lord's heart to have His house arranged properly with orderly behavior in the house and implies the ability of the house members to give and take orders.

A Disorderly House

In 2 Thessalonians 3:7, Paul writes, "For yourselves know how ye ought to follow us: for we behaved not ourselves disorderly among you…." He continues in Verse 11, "For we hear that there are some which walk among you disorderly, working not at all, but are busybodies." In a disorderly house, the members display an ungodly character that results in improper behavior, which is the opposite of orderly ones.

The *Vines* translates orderly as "an adjective that signifies decency, modesty, and of good behavior." Paul, writing to the young pastor Timothy, said, "These things write I unto thee, hoping to come unto thee shortly: But if I tarry long, that thou mayest know how thou oughtest to behave thyself in the house of God, which is the church of the living God, the pillar and ground of the truth" (1 Timothy

3:14-15). He instructed the pastor on acceptable and unacceptable behaviors in the house of God.

Out of Order

Ezekiel 37 illustrates a disorderly house. In the Spirit, the Lord reveals a valley full of bones to the prophet Ezekiel. In Verse 11, the Lord discloses that this represented His house, saying, "Then he said unto me, Son of man, these bones are the whole house of Israel." We often follow the narrative as the Lord has Ezekiel to prophesy in order for the bones to live. However, let us look at what happened to the bones that caused them to be this way in the first place.

A closer look at what the Lord said in Ezekiel 37:11 will bear this out. It says, "Then he said unto me, Son of man, these bones are the whole house of Israel: behold, they say, Our bones are dried, and our hope is lost: we are cut off for our parts." Notice it does not say what the Lord said, but what they said. This is why some churches are dry, dislocated, and disconnected. According to the Word of God, a member who is not connected and serving will become dry and disconnected and eventually be dislocated and destroyed by the enemy.

Thank God they got back in order when the man of God spoke the Word to them. They stood up as an "exceeding great army" (Verse 10), which depicts the church arranged in an orderly manner, ready to take orders and carry out the commands of the Lord. In Verse 17, the Lord says, "And join them one to another into one stick; and they shall become one in my hand." A church that is in order will inevitably be a victorious body of believers.

"Good order is the foundation of all things."
EDMUND BURKE

SHOW THE HOUSE TO THE HOUSE

The Unity of the House

5

"Endeavouring to keep the unity of the Spirit in the bond of peace."

Ephesians 4:3 (KJV)

In Ephesians 4:3, the word *unity* is the neuter of the Greek word *heis*, which means "one." Jesus used this same word in John 10:30, saying, "I and my Father are one," and again in John 17:11b, "Holy Father, keep through thine own name those whom thou hast given me, that they may be one, as we are." Later, while praying for the disciples, Jesus declares:

> Neither pray I for these alone, but for them also which shall believe on me through their word; That they all may be *one*; as thou, Father, art in me, and I in thee, that they also may be *one* in us: that the world may believe that thou hast sent me. And the glory which thou gavest me I have given them; that they may be *one*, even as we are *one*: I in them, and thou

in me, that they may be made perfect in *one*; and that the world may know that thou hast sent me, and hast loved them, as thou hast loved me.

JOHN 17:20-23 (EMPHASIS ADDED)

Agreement and Harmony

Metaphorically speaking, the concept of one symbolizes a union or concord or to be joined together in agreement and harmony. Therefore, Jesus emphasized that we, the church, would be united in the Lord, displaying the spirit of agreement and walking in harmony. It goes without saying that there can be unity with no agreement or harmony. This can be observed in many of today's marriages, with couples united in matrimony, but divorce is looming because of the lack of agreement or harmony. Plainly stated, you can tie a cat's tail to that of a dog, and they will be in unity, but there will be no agreement or harmony!

Dwelling in Unity

Behold, how good and how pleasant it is for brethren to dwell together in unity! It is like the precious ointment upon the head, that ran down upon the beard, even Aaron's beard: that went down to the skirts of his garments; As the dew of Hermon, and as the dew that descended upon the mountains of Zion: for there the LORD commanded the blessing, even life for evermore.

Psalm 133:1-3

In this text, David delineates how to ensure the blessing is forever, and the principle of spiritual unity does it. David illustrates this concept by portraying a body, which refers to the body of Christ or the church.

Anointing Upon the Head

First, David paints a picture of the anointing flowing from the head. Paul speaks of the head in 1 Corinthians 11:3, saying, "But I would have you know, that the head of every man is Christ; and the head of the woman is the man; and the head of Christ is God." In correlation to marriage, he says in Ephesians 5:23, "For the husband is the head of the wife, even as Christ is the head of the church: and he is the saviour of the body." He further conveys in Colossians 1:18, "And he (Christ) is the head of the body, the church...." David suggests that the anointing flows to the beard, which means it gets on the neck. Most of us will agree that the pastor is not the head of the local church but that he is the connection between the head (Jesus Christ) and the local body (congregation). Thus, the first reference to beard bespeaks of the neck, which is the pastor.

Anointing Upon the Shoulders

David then mentions "Aaron's beard," which refers to the elders. This also points toward the shoulders, which support the neck and the head. Isaiah wrote, "for unto us a child is born, unto us a son is given: and the government shall be upon his shoulders..." (Isaiah 9:6). The elders are the government of the local church and, therefore, are depicted as the shoulders. Of course, the deacons and the rest of the local church leadership are included as the arms and hands extending from the shoulders.

Anointing Upon the Body

David adds the finishing touches by saying the anointing flows down as the dew of Hermon descends upon the mountains of Zion. Most of us will agree that Zion usually refers to the church or the rest of the members of the congregation. Note Hebrews 12:22-23, "But ye are come unto mount Sion (Zion), and unto the city of the living God, the heavenly Jerusalem, and to an innumerable company of angels, To the general assembly and church of the firstborn...."

David concludes by purporting that the blessing of the Lord is forever commanded upon the church, manifesting unity, agreement and harmony.

Committed to the Lord and Connected to Leadership

It is a foregone conclusion and without argument that Jesus is the one and only head of the body of Christ, the church. However, the mention of the head in Scripture has a double reference. What I mean by this is you cannot make mention of the head and leave out the neck. There is no head without a neck. The neck connects the rest of the body to the head. The pastor is not the head, but he is the leader of the local church. Many refer to the pastor as the under-shepherd, implying he can only lead as he follows the true leader, Jesus Christ.

The Pastor is the Neck

I point this out because many people profess a commitment to the Lord but don't have any connection with leadership or their pastor. Some members of the body don't have a pastor at all! Imagine a body without a neck. It can still function but with many limitations. Furthermore, imagine a head trying to go somewhere, and the body won't follow. During Moses' time, God called the Israelites a "stiff-necked" people, which meant they wanted to be committed to the Lord but not by the connection of their neck, Moses. This provoked God to get rid of them and give Moses another people, but like a good neck (pastor), Moses stayed connected to the rest of the body (congregation) and interceded on their behalf.

The Lord and the Leader

We find a brilliant demonstration of this commitment in 2 Kings 2. Elijah and Elisha are about to part ways, and Elijah directs his son in the faith to stay put as he goes from Gilgal to Jordan. We pick up the narrative in Verse 2, "And Elijah said unto Elisha, Tarry here, I pray thee; for the LORD hath sent me to Bethel. And Elisha said unto him, As the LORD liveth, and as thy soul liveth, I will not leave thee. So they went down to Bethel." At each juncture, Elijah directed him to stay, and each time, Elisha gave the same response (see Verses 4 and 6). I am making the point that Elisha was committed to the LORD and connected to his leader.

A Divine Connection

For this reason, I assert that church unity begins with a commitment to the Lord and a connection with the pastor and other church leadership and continues with a connection with fellow members of the local church body. The Lord expects the local church leadership and membership to be of "one mind and one accord" or on the "same sheet of music." This can only be achieved when all people incorporate and embrace the tenets of unity.

Tenets of Church Unity

As I mentioned before, biblical unity means one, carrying the connotation of agreement and harmony. It also offers the thought of the same. The Greek word for *same* is *autos*, which means "one, the same, alike, or bearing some resemblance." The following list provides ten biblical principles that will aid and assist churches in maintaining a Spirit of Unity. This list is not meant to be exhaustive or all-inclusive but sufficient enough that, if followed, the pastor, leadership and membership will remain in agreement, harmony, and ultimately in unity.

1 | The Same Spirit of Faith

> *"We having the same spirit of faith, according as it is written, I believed, and therefore have I spoken; we also believe, and therefore speak...."*
>
> 2 Corinthians 4:13 (KJV)

This principle speaks to what we believe. It is as easy A-B-C. Firstly, A stands for As it is written. It must first be written in the Holy Scriptures for us to have the authority to believe and speak it. Jesus demonstrated this in Luke 4 when he resisted the devil with the Word of God. Each time, Jesus responded with "It is written" according to specific scriptures in the Bible. His first response was, "It is written, That man shall not live by bread alone, but by every word of God" (Verse 4), which can be found in Deuteronomy 8:3. His second response was, "Get thee behind me, Satan: for it is written, Thou shalt worship the Lord thy God, and him only shalt thou serve" (Verse 8), which can be found in Exodus 34:14, Deuteronomy 6:13 and 10:20. Jesus' final response was, "It is said, Thou shalt not tempt the Lord thy God" (Verse 12), located in Deuteronomy 6:16. Paul said, "Be ye followers of me, even as I also am of Christ" (1 Corinthians 11:1). Jesus set a sterling example for us to follow.

Secondly, B stands for Believe what is written in the Scriptures. We must know what is written and continually hear what is written before we can believe what is written. Romans 10:17 says, "So then faith cometh by hearing, and hearing by the word of God."

Lastly, C stands for Confess or speak what is written in the Word of God. Jesus taught this principle in Mark 11:23, "For verily I say unto you, that whosoever shall say unto this mountain, be thou removed, and be thou cast into the sea; and shall not doubt in his heart, but shall believe that those things which he saith shall come to pass; he shall have whatsoever he saith." The bottom line is we must believe it before we speak it in order for the Lord to perform it.

2 | The Same Spirit

> *"Now there are diversities of gifts, but the same Spirit."*
>
> 1 CORINTHIANS 12:4 (KJV)

Having the same Spirit bespeaks of allowing the witness and work of the Holy Spirit to empower and lead us because He is the One Who works in us "both to will and to do according to his good pleasure" (Philippians 2:13). The Bible declares that Caleb had another spirit because he followed the Lord wholly (Numbers 14:24). Daniel displayed an excellent spirit when he prayed despite being threatened with death (Daniel 6:3). Stephen possessed an irresistible spirit while facing judgment from the Sanhedrin courts (Acts 6:10). It would behoove us to be filled with the Holy Spirit living in us so we can all walk and live in the power of the same Spirit.

3 | The Same Mind

> *"Now I beseech you, brethren, by the name of our Lord Jesus Christ, that ye all speak the same thing, and that there be no divisions among you; but that ye be perfectly joined together in the same mind and in the same judgment."*
>
> 1 CORINTHIANS 1:10 (KJV)

According to 1 Corinthians 2:16, we all have the mind of Christ. The same mind describes those who have one common vision, purpose, and counsel. The leader receives the vision and purpose through the counsel of the Lord, writes it down and preaches it, and the leadership and membership must catch and run with it (Habakkuk 2:2). This causes us to have the same focus and to all be moving in the same direction.

4 | Speak the Same Thing

> *"Now I beseech you, brethren, by the name of our Lord Jesus Christ, that ye all speak the same thing, and that there be no divisions among you; but that ye be perfectly joined together in the same mind and in the same judgment."*
>
> 1 CORINTHIANS 1:10 (KJV)

Again, Jesus set a perfect example of this principle when he declared, "For I have not spoken of myself; but the Father which sent me, he gave me a commandment, what I should say, and what I should speak" (John 12:49). In a real sense, this is how the principle of confession works. The word *confession* is a Greek compound word of *homo*, meaning "the same," and *logeo*, meaning "to speak." It means to speak the same thing that the Father speaks. Jesus demonstrated this. After all, He is the Apostle and High Priest of our profession (confession), according to Hebrews 3:1. So if He is under commandment to speak what the Father speaks, then so are we!

5 | The Same Steps

> *"I desired Titus, and with him I sent a brother. Did Titus make a gain of you? walked we not in the same spirit? walked we not in the same steps?"*
>
> 2 CORINTHIANS 12:18 (KJV)

Paul alluded that he and Titus did things the same way. This is made possible by establishing standard operating procedures (SOP) that are put in place to ensure that everyone knows and follows the same instructions and ultimately does things in the same manner. Paul writes in Philippians 3:17, "Brethren, be followers together of me, and mark them which walk so as ye have us for an ensample." An example displays, allowing you to see someone doing something. An ensample takes an example a little further by showing you how and letting you practice doing it the same way or with the same steps.

6 | The Same Rule

> *"Nevertheless, whereto we have already attained, let us walk by the same rule, let us mind the same thing."*
>
> PHILIPPIANS 3:16 (KJV)

The concept of rule indicates standards, rules, or boundaries. The same rule connotes all of us being under the rule of the Word of God. Like the Word of God, rules or standards never change.

Therefore, continuing in the things we know and have learned will allow the Lord to raise the standard and give us a "more excellent way" of doing things.

7 | The Same Love

> *"If there be therefore any consolation in Christ, if any comfort of love, if any fellowship of the Spirit, if any bowels and mercies, Fulfil ye my joy, that ye be likeminded, having the same love, being of one accord, of one mind. Let nothing be done through strife or vainglory; but in lowliness of mind let each esteem other better than themselves."*
>
> Philippians 2:1-3 (KJV)

In 1 John 4:7-8, John writes, "Beloved, let us love one another: for love is of God; and every one that loveth is born of God, and knoweth God. He that loveth not knoweth not God; for God is love." A church that manifests the love of God displays the very nature of God. Love must be the primary motivation for everything that takes place in the house of the Lord. John further says in 1 John 2:10, "He that loveth his brother abideth in the light, and there is none occasion of stumbling in him." As long as the Holy Spirit is allowed to flow freely in the church, this will not be difficult because "the love of God is shed abroad in our hearts by the Holy Spirit" (Romans 5:5).

8 | The Same Earnest Care

> "But thanks be to God, which put the same earnest care into the heart of Titus for you."
>
> 2 CORINTHIANS 8:16 (KJV)

Exhibiting the same earnest care advocates having the same concern and affection consistently for every member, visitor, and friend. James 2:9 says, "But if ye have respect to persons, ye commit sin, and are convinced of the law as transgressors." We must not forget that God never shows respect for one person above another (Romans 2:11).

9 | The Same Judgment

> "Now I beseech you, brethren, by the name of our Lord Jesus Christ, that ye all speak the same thing, and that there be no divisions among you; but that ye be perfectly joined together in the same mind and in the same judgment."
>
> 1 CORINTHIANS 1:10 (KJV)

In the simplest form, we display the same judgment when submitting to the Word of God and the church leadership. This means that we trust the spiritual discernment of the leadership, and we willingly and prayerfully follow their decisions.

10 | The Same Diligence

> *"And we desire that every one of you do shew the same diligence to the full assurance of hope unto the end: That ye be not slothful, but followers of them who through faith and patience inherit the promises."*
>
> Hebrews 6:11-12 (KJV)

Diligence means "zeal, fervency or fire." It represents an eagerness or haste in everything that we do. In essence, we "go hard" every time because we are all on fire. The same diligence ultimately flows from an excellent spirit. Excellence does not mean perfect or without flaws. It does not mean doing something without mistakes. Excellence comes from inward motivation, not outward observation, which means the Holy Spirit motivates you to make the same effort every time. He causes you to consistently give nothing but your very best in your service unto the Lord. This same diligence causes a ministry to be one of excellence in every aspect.

"Alone we can do so little; together we can do so much."

Helen Keller

The Treasury of the House

6

"And they burnt the city with fire, and all that was therein: only the silver, and the gold, and the vessels of brass and of iron, they put into the treasury of the house of the LORD."

JOSHUA 6:24 (KJV)

The Lord's house is often the most neglected and under-appreciated place where the people of God are concerned. This is a "crying shame," especially when the Lord has been so good to us! This was David's dilemma as he surveyed the house of God. God had blessed him abundantly, and his house was made of the best materials and encompassed the finest things money could buy while the Lord's house paled in comparison. The Lord's house consisted of nothing more than a collapsible tent they carried everywhere they went.

Contributing to the House

Notwithstanding, David decided to do something about it and

declared in 1 Chronicles 29:3, "Moreover, because I have set my affection to the house of my God, I have of mine own proper good, of gold and silver, which I have given to the house of my God, over and above all that I have prepared for the holy house." David gave millions of dollars toward the building of the Lord's house. The chief of the fathers and leaders of the tribes immediately followed David's example in 1 Chronicles 29:6 (*Holy Bible, New Living Translation*), "Then the family leaders, the leaders of the tribes of Israel, the generals and captains of the army, and the king's administrative officers all gave willingly. For the construction of the Temple of God, they gave almost 188 tons of gold, 10,000 gold coins, about 375 tons of silver, about 675 tons of bronze, and about 3,750 tons of iron." In Verse 9, we find even the people of the kingdom joining in: "Then the people rejoiced, for that they offered willingly, because with perfect hearts they offered willingly to the LORD: and David the king also rejoiced with great joy."

Divine Owner and Provider

David and the people gave joyfully and generously because they recognized the Lord as the Owner and Provider of all they possessed. They gratefully and thankfully blessed the LORD, saying, "Thine, O LORD, is the greatness, and the power, and the glory, and the victory, and the majesty: for all that is in the heaven and in the earth is thine;

thine is the kingdom, O LORD, and thou art exalted as head above all. Both riches and honour come of thee, and thou reignest over all; and in thine hand is power and might; and in thine hand it is to make great, and to give strength unto all" (1 Chronicles 29:11-12). Glory to God!

Building the Lord's House

In many churches, we are facing the same dilemma that David faced, and I believe it is one of the main reasons that ministries cannot make ends meet and fall far short of the intended purpose the Lord has for them. This is revealed in Haggai 1:2-4, "Thus speaketh the LORD of hosts, saying, This people say, The time is not come, the time that the LORD's house should be built. Then came the word of the LORD by Haggai the prophet, saying, Is it time for you, O ye, to dwell in your ceiled houses, and this house lie waste?" This is very familiar to David's era. The people were "living large" while the Lord's house was dilapidated.

Consider Your Ways

Haggai continued prophesying in Verse 5, saying, "Now therefore thus saith the LORD of hosts; Consider your ways." He continues by telling them that this is why they were not experiencing the increase and prosperity that the Lord promised: "Ye have sown much, and bring in little; ye eat, but ye have not enough; ye drink, but ye are not filled with drink; ye clothe you, but there is none warm; and he that earneth wages earneth wages to put it into a bag with holes" (Verse 6).

Problem Solved

The Lord then gives them the only way to rectify this problem in Verse 8, "Go up to the mountain, and bring wood, and build the house; and I will take pleasure in it, and I will be glorified, saith the LORD." When He says, I will be glorified when you "bring wood" to build, spiritually speaking, He is talking about financial resources or money, just as He used the word *meat* when referring to the *tithe* in Malachi 3. David understood this and brought the money necessary to fund the building of the Lord's house.

All Money Belongs to God

Notice what the Lord says later in Haggai 2:8-9, "The silver is mine, and the gold is mine, saith the LORD of hosts. The glory of this latter house shall be greater than of the former, saith the LORD of hosts: and in this place will I give peace, saith the LORD of hosts." I am alluding to the fact that the house of the Lord is to be built and sustained based on tithes, offerings, and vows. This financial investment was neglected in Haggai's day, so the Lord commanded, "Consider your ways!" Remember that the essence of this is His ownership and our stewardship.

Tithes, Offerings and Vows

Pay close attention to what the Lord says in Deuteronomy 12:5-7:

> But unto *the place* (Lord's house) which the LORD your God shall choose out of all your tribes to put his name there, even unto *his habitation* shall ye seek, and thither thou shalt come: And thither ye shall bring your burnt offerings, and your sacrifices, and *your tithes*, and *heave offerings* of your hand, and *your vows*, and your *freewill offerings*, and the firstlings of your herds and of your flocks: And there ye shall eat before the LORD your God, and ye shall rejoice in all that ye put your hand unto, *ye* and *your households*, wherein the LORD thy God hath blessed thee.

In sum, if you bring the tithes, offerings, and vows for the building of the Lord's house, He will abundantly bless your house.

Bring All the Tithes

"Will a man rob God? Yet ye have robbed me. But ye say, Wherein have we robbed thee? In tithes and offerings. Ye are cursed with a curse: for ye have robbed me, even this whole nation."

MALACHI 3:8-9 (KJV)

This is the same indictment that the Lord had against the people that Haggai was addressing. Remember, He said they were basically cursed because of their neglect toward the funding of the Lord's house, and therefore, had bags with holes and could not keep their wages or money (Haggai 1:5). In this text, the Lord declares that they not only robbed Him but the whole nation or the people of God. Notice also that the Lord says they robbed Him in tithes and offerings. But in Verse 10, He commands, "Bring ye all the tithes into the storehouse." We will discover this reason as we discuss the tithe in more detail.

What is the tithe?

The word *tithe* means "tenth." It implies a tenth of all and on all. Simply put, the tithe is ten percent of the whole or gross. The tithe is the beginning of giving. It is the floor where you begin, not the ceiling where you end. The Lord said tithe and made no mention of the offering because the tithe is considered the first fruit. The tithe also represents the first tenth or what many would call "right off the top." Therefore, if you don't bring the tithe first, then the rest is cursed. Some people say, "I can't afford to tithe." The truth is you can't afford not to tithe! Some ask, "Do I pay tithe or give tithe?" The answer is based upon your revelation. Most people pay their bills reluctantly, but we must give the tithe willingly and cheerfully.

Jacob had an encounter with God using what is known as the vision of "Jacob's ladder" (Genesis 28). At the end of this encounter, Jacob declares, "And this stone, which I have set for a pillar, shall be God's house, and of all that thou shalt give me I will surely give the tenth (tithe) unto thee" (Genesis 28:22). What is vitally important to note is that the tithe belongs to the Lord, and to keep it is to steal from Him. Leviticus 27:30 bears this out: "And all the tithe of the land, whether of the seed of the land, or the fruit of the tree, is the LORD's: it is holy unto the LORD."

Tithing and the Law

Some well-meaning people teach that the tithe was a part of the Mosaic Law; therefore, it is unnecessary to practice. The problem with this notion is that it is contrary to the Scriptures. The Bible records that Cain brought God an offering from the fruit of the ground, and Abel brought the firstlings (tithe) of his flock. God respected Abel's tithe but did not accept Cain's offering (Genesis 4).

Abraham gave tithes of all unto Melchizedek in Genesis 14:20. In Genesis 28, Jacob promised to surely give the tenth (tithes) of all he received, as long as the Lord supplied him with protection, bread, and raiment (clothing). These accounts were from many generations before Moses was born and long before The Law was instituted.

When is the Tithe Required?

> *"Bring ye all the tithes into the storehouse, that there may be meat in mine house, and prove me now herewith, saith the LORD of hosts, if I will not open you the windows of heaven, and pour you out a blessing, that there shall not be room enough to receive it."*
>
> Malachi 3:10 (KJV)

The adverb now indicates urgency. It signifies that whenever God has blessed you with income or an increase, you should tithe immediately or as soon as possible. Proverbs 3:9-10 makes this clear: "Honour the LORD with thy substance, and with the first fruits of all thine increase: So shall thy barns be filled with plenty, and thy presses shall burst out with new wine." The implication is that if you honor Him with the tithe now, you shall receive the blessing now.

Where does the Tithe go?

> *"Bring ye all the tithes into the storehouse, that there may be meat in mine house, and prove me now herewith, saith the LORD of hosts, if I will not open you the windows of heaven, and pour you out a blessing, that there shall not be room enough to receive it."*
>
> MALACHI 3:10 (KJV)

Notice: He does not say to send all the tithes but to bring them into the storehouse. This is because the tithe should be brought to the house of God, where you are a member and are being fed the Word of God. This is critical to understand because sending the tithe to support a ministry that is not your home church is erroneous. Please know that I am not against the support of anyone's ministry. Simply put, the tithe goes to the church where you are connected. Of course, sometimes, we are not physically located near our home church. In those cases, it is okay to send it there. The main purpose of the tithe is to meet the needs of the house of God, of which you are a member.

Reasons to Tithe

> *"Bring ye all the tithes into the storehouse, that there may be meat in mine house, and prove me now herewith, saith the LORD of hosts, if I will not open you the windows of heaven,*

and pour you out a blessing, that there shall not be room enough to receive it. And I will rebuke the devourer for your sakes, and he shall not destroy the fruits of your ground; neither shall your vine cast her fruit before the time in the field, saith the LORD of hosts. And all nations shall call you blessed: for ye shall be a delightsome land, saith the LORD of hosts."

MALACHI 3:10-12 (KJV)

The Lord has promised the faithful tither an open heaven, an abundance of blessing where He would rebuke the devour (the devil), which comes in the form of recession, inflation, high prices, drawdowns, layoffs, setbacks, and cutbacks (to name a few), and provide protection for the fruit in your life. He promises divine favor among the nations, which includes those who consider themselves your enemies, and overall protection from the curse and the evil that plagues the land!

Bring an Offering

According to Malachi 3, there is a difference between tithes and offerings. We have discovered that the tithes are a requirement that the Lord considers as His, and there are serious consequences for withholding it from Him. While tithing is an act of obedience, an offering is a sacrifice or a gesture of love. It is to bring God a present, to offer or give Him something because of your gratefulness and thankfulness. Giving God an offering is like saying, "Here's a little something extra," or "Lord, I just want you to have this." Offering is what you do above and beyond the requirement to tithe. Psalms 96:8 says, "Give unto the LORD the glory due unto his name: bring an offering, and come into his courts."

Obedience or Sacrifice

Some often give God offerings and never get around to tithing. I submit to you that this is an error far from pleasing unto God. Samuel said unto Saul, "Behold to obey is better than sacrifice" (1 Samuel 15:22). Saul, attempting to appease God with an offering instead of pleasing Him with obedience, thought his gift would appease the Lord's anger. He discovered the hard way that an offering or gift of any kind does not substitute for the requirement of obedience to God. David said, "For thou desires not sacrifice; else would I give it; thou delightest not in burnt offering" (Psalm 51:16). David knew that, much like tithing, he had to repent for what he had done and obey, and there was nothing he could offer in the place of that. The offering is something that you bring in addition to the tithe. The offering starts with a presentation of your heart to the Lord.

Making Vows to God

"Vow and pay to the Lord your God; let all who are round about Him bring presents to Him Who ought to be [reverently] feared."
PSALMS 76:11 (AMPC)

Vowing is a covenant concept we don't hear preached very often, but it is very common in the Old Testament. A vow is a promise to do or give something, a gift graciously bestowed. Vowing is not a pledge or a negotiation with the Lord; it is a promise of commitment or a proclamation of a binding agreement.

The Seriousness of the Vow

Before plunging into the principle of vowing, let me admonish anyone who is not a faithful tither or has yet to begin to give offerings above the tithe. You should not, I repeat, you should not fiddle around with the vow if you are not a committed tither. Making a vow is such a serious undertaking that it is better not to fool with it at all than to vow and not be able to fulfill your promise. Ecclesiastes 5:4-5 warns: "When thou vowest a vow unto God, defer not to pay it; for he hath no pleasure in fools: pay that which thou hast vowed. Better is it that thou shouldest not vow, than that thou shouldest vow and not pay." Unlike the tithe, the word *pay* does apply in the case of the vow; it becomes a debt owed.

Hannah's Vow

In the book of First Samuel, there is a superb example of the vow in action in Chapter 1. The story starts with a man named Elkanah and his two wives, Peninnah and Hannah. Peninnah had children, and Hannah had none because her womb was shut up. As Hannah cried and prayed unto the Lord, Verse 11 says, "And she vowed a vow." Hannah was in a crisis and desperately needed the Lord to move in her life, which is a good reason to vow. Hannah was in a position to release her faith in God, who could do what was impossible for man. Hannah promised that if God would give her a manchild (Verse 11), she would give him back to the Lord to serve Him all the days of his life. Long story short, the priest Eli observed Hannah praying and pronounced in Verse 17, "Go in peace: and the God of Israel grant thee thy petition that thou hast asked of him."

As previously stated, a vow is a promise to do or give something graciously. It is a commitment and a binding agreement. The reason this is significant is because the Lord is a Promise Keeper. He will always fulfill His end of the agreement. The question is, "Will you keep your promise to Him?" Many times, a vow is a promise to give something you don't have if the Lord will give it to you first or to do something you have never done if the Lord will do something for you. In vowing, you expect God to bring it or do it, and He expects you to do the same. When you vow, you are saying, "Lord, I trust you to keep Your word," and the Lord replies, "Can I trust you to keep yours?" this is not for the casual Christian. Your word must mean something to you and the Lord!

We pick up the narrative in 1 Samuel 1:19, "… and Elkanah knew Hannah his wife; and the LORD remembered her." The Lord remembered the vow she had made in faith, and in Verse 20, Hannah conceived and called his name Samuel, saying, "Because I have asked him of the LORD." The Lord fulfilled His end of the agreement; it was time for Hannah to fulfill hers. She was a woman who understood vowing as it related to the covenant. She was well aware of the seriousness of the vows according to Deuteronomy 23:21, "When thou shalt vow a vow unto the LORD thy God, thou shalt not slack to pay it: for the LORD thy God will surely require it of thee; and it would be sin in thee."

As the story continues, Hannah weaned Samuel before releasing him to the Lord. In 1 Samuel 1:26-28, she tells Eli:

> Oh my Lord, as thy soul liveth, my Lord, I am the woman that stood by thee here, praying unto the LORD. For this child I prayed; and the LORD hath given me my petition which I asked of him: Therefore also I have lent him to the LORD; as long as he liveth

he shall be lent to the LORD. And he worshipped the LORD there.

Because this was a personal commitment between Hannah and the Lord, she did not allow Elkanah to deliver Samuel to the Lord; she wanted to pay her vow to the Lord personally.

Kingdom Investments

All in all, when it comes to the vow and every other form of giving, the words to the song ring true: "You can't beat God giving no matter how hard you try!" Hannah, whose womb was shut up before the vow, asked for one child. But after she fulfilled her vow, 1 Samuel 2:21 says, "And the LORD visited Hannah, so that she conceived, and bare three sons and two daughters. And the child Samuel grew before the LORD." When we give our tithes, offerings, and vows into the treasury of the Lord's house, we make divine investments into the kingdom of our God. As a result, the rate of return on our kingdom investments will be supernatural, according to Luke 6:38, "Give, and it shall be given unto you; good measure, pressed down, and shaken together, and running over, shall men give into your bosom…." Praise the Lord, somebody!

SHOW THE HOUSE TO THE HOUSE

"Remember that the happiest people are not those getting more, but those giving more."
H. JACKSON BROWN JR.

The Healthy Church

"But speaking the truth in love, may grow up into him in all things, which is the head, even Christ: From whom the whole body fitly joined together and compacted by that which every joint supplieth, according to the effectual working in the measure of every part, maketh increase of the body unto the edifying of itself in love."

EPHESIANS 4:15-16 (KJV)

In the Bible, the human body is frequently used as a symbol to depict the spiritual body of Christ. This comparison often delineates how a healthy church grows, like a healthy physical body. Like the human anatomy, this growth process occurs as the body parts stay connected to the head and function in concert with the rest of the body. In contrast, the Church must maintain the vital connection with our Head, Jesus Christ, and the other members to produce abundant and long-lasting church growth. The Apostle Paul exhorts that we may "grow up into him in all things, which is the head, even Christ" (Ephesians 4:15). With that said, the focus of the

Church should not be on church growth, per se, because like the physical body, a healthy church will ultimately culminate in fruitful church growth.

Connected Members

> *"From whom the whole body fitly joined together and compacted by that which every joint supplieth, according to the effectual working in the measure of every part, maketh increase of the body unto the edifying of itself in love."*
> Ephesians 4:16 (KJV) Emphasis Added

The phrase *fitly joined together* means "to fit or frame together, be fitly framed, or joined closely together." Metaphorically, it bespeaks of various parts of the Church as a building. The phrase also carries the connotation that we are perfectly connected or assembled. It is much like the classic children's song, "Dem Bones," which I learned as a child: "The toe bone's connected to the foot bone, the foot bone's connected to the ankle bone, the ankle bone's connected to the leg bone," and so on. Thus, each member must be assembled correctly and connected in its rightful place. First Corinthians 12:27 says, "Now ye are the body of Christ, and members in particular."

The Scriptures record, "If the foot shall say, Because I am not the hand, I am not of the body; is it therefore not of the body?" (1

Corinthians 12:15). The obvious answer is "no;" it is the Spirit of the Lord who decides what body part you are and, ultimately, sets "the members every one of them in the body, as it hath pleased him" (1 Corinthians 12:18). When we are perfectly connected in this way, it is like bone marrow, which fosters strength, soundness, and health within the members of the body. Thus, each member is positioned to function interdependently and poised to help foster growth within the whole body. As members of the Church, we must stay connected to grow individually and ensure the growth of the church body as a whole.

Committed Members

> *"From whom the whole body **fitly** joined together and **compacted** by that which every joint supplieth, according to the effectual working in the measure of every part, maketh increase of the body unto the edifying of itself in love."*
> EPHESIANS 4:16 (KJV) EMPHASIS ADDED

The Greek word for *compacted* is *sumbibazo*, which means "to unite, to knit, or knit together." It suggests something interwoven and cannot be separated or taken apart easily. The word *compacted* implies faithfulness and loyalty between the head and members of the body. It is a foregone conclusion that Jesus Christ, our Head, is faithful in every way. He is trustworthy, reliable, and loyal until the end, declaring, "I will never leave thee, nor forsake thee" (Hebrews 13:5), and "lo, I am with you always, even unto the end of the world" (Matthew 28:20). However, the members must not only be connected but also be faithfully committed for the body to function correctly.

Paul admonishes in 1 Corinthians 4:2, "Moreover it is required in stewards, that a man be found faithful." The Lord expects the members to be compacted, committed, or faithful because it is essential to the health and ultimate growth of the body. David says of the Lord, "Mine eyes shall be upon the faithful of the land, that they may dwell with me: he that walketh in a perfect way, he shall serve me." (Psalm 101:6). Solomon writes, "Most men will proclaim everyone his own goodness: but a faithful man who can find?" (Proverbs 20:6). The Lord is looking for the members of His body to be faithful.

Now, let me point out that some people consider a member faithful just because he or she attends most of the church services and events. This does not necessarily mean that the person is faithful. A "Faith-full" member is full of FAITH (Forward Action in Trusting Him), trustworthy, reliable, dependable, and loyal. Someone once said, "A loyal member is FAT (Faithful, Available, and Teachable). FAT members can be depended upon to remain teachable, always available, and diligently release their faith by serving in the house of the Lord.

Contributing Members

*"From whom the whole body fitly joined together and compacted **by that which every joint supplieth, according to the effectual working in the measure of every part**, maketh increase of the body unto the edifying of itself in love."*
EPHESIANS 4:16 (KJV) EMPHASIS ADDED

In this text, the joint represents the member that supplies or contributes its part to the body. The same verse in the *Amplified Bible, Classic Edition*, says, "For because of Him the whole body (the church, in all its various parts), closely joined and firmly knit together by the joints and ligaments with which it is supplied, when each part [with power adapted to its need] is working properly [in all its functions], grows to full maturity, building itself up in love."

In Hebrews 4:12, the writer uses the terms *joints* and *marrow* because the joints are the bones, and the marrow is the jelly-like substance within the bones that reproduces the blood. The marrow carries the nutrients from one joint to another to ensure the bones are healthy, strong, fat, and able to grow properly. Writing to the Colossians, Paul explains, "And not holding the Head, from which all the body by joints and bands having nourishment ministered, and knit together, increaseth with the increase of God" (Colossians 2:19). However, when a bone is out of joint or out of place, the flow of marrow is inhibited, causing the marrow and bones to dry up. Consequently, the bones become brittle and fragile, and they run the risk of breaking. The same goes for when a member is dislocated and out of place; that church body becomes weak, fragile, and unhealthy. A church body in this condition cannot and will not grow.

Consider the illustration of the man with the withered hand in Mark 3:1-5. This man's hand was withered because it lacked sufficient marrow and moisture. Accordingly, the bones in his hand had become dry, weak, and malnourished. As a result, his hand was desiccated, pining away, and withered. The withered-hand man could not extend his hand and, therefore, could not touch or fully embrace his community. In essence, the man was handicapped and helpless, looking for a helping hand instead of extending one. This is not to say that every handicapped person is helpless. Many handicapped people have overcome by compensating for it in other ways. Conversely, some helpless members help less and, therefore, cause the Church to be handicapped. With a withered hand, the Church cannot embrace its community, city, or the world we have been commanded to reach.

For this reason, Jesus Christ came to make the crooked things straight. He commanded the withered-hand man to stand and straighten out his hand. Essentially, Jesus healed the man so he would no longer withhold the support he should have been giving. When the man stretched out his hand, it became a healthy and functioning joint that could now fully embrace those around him. Jesus is doing the same with the church body, commanding us to stretch out our hands of support and become healthy joints, functioning properly and contributing to the growth of the body of Christ.

Causing the Body to Grow

> *"From whom the whole body fitly joined together and compacted by that which every joint supplieth, according to the effectual working in the measure of every part, **maketh increase of the body** unto the edifying of itself in love."*
> Ephesians 4:16 (KJV) Emphasis Added

The word *increase* here means "to grow naturally and spiritually." It implies increasing in every aspect and in every way. Pay close attention to Ephesians 4:15b in the *Amplified Bible, Classic Edition*, "Enfolded in love, let us grow up in every way and in all things into Him Who is the Head, [even] Christ (the Messiah, the Anointed One)." The *New American Standard Bible* says this: "…we are to grow up in all aspects into Him who is the head, even Christ…." The bottom line is a strong and healthy church will inevitably grow in stature, substance, and, eventually, in sum. Remember, God is more interested in building big people than simply having a big church.

"Church health is related more to the growth in maturity of the members and attendees than numerical metrics such as attendance and giving."
PASTOR RICK WARREN

The Holy Spirit's Ministry   8

"And when he had said this, he breathed on them, and saith unto them, Receive ye the Holy Ghost...."

JOHN 20:22 (KJV)

After His resurrection, Jesus walked through closed doors, stood in the midst of His disciples, and made the following statement: "Peace be unto you: as my Father hath sent me, even so send I you. And when he had said this, he breathed on them, and saith unto them, Receive ye the Holy Ghost...." Many ask, "Is this when they received the Holy Ghost?" Most of us will agree that the answer is an obvious "no" in light of Acts 2. We know they did not receive the person of the Holy Ghost until after Jesus ascended right before their very eyes. The Disciples went into the upper room at His command and did not experience the outpouring until the day of Pentecost (50 days after He rose from the dead).

Jesus himself declared, "It is expedient for you that I go away: for if I go not away, the Comforter (Holy Ghost) will not come unto you; but if I depart, I will send him unto you" (John 16:7b). So, what was

Jesus saying in this text? I submit to you that when He breathed on them, He inspired them with the desire to receive the Holy Ghost's ministry. In other words, Jesus placed the desire within them, producing an expectation to receive the ministry of the Holy Spirit. Better yet, He wanted them to receive and allow the full operation of the Holy Spirit to function in every aspect and in every way.

In many churches today, the operation of the Holy Spirit is very little or nonexistent. Many churches either don't believe in the Holy Spirit's ministry or relegate His ministry to something that took place "once upon a time." The results have been devastating, to say the least. Churches everywhere have become nothing more than social clubs where the power of God is not present or expected. This is so unfortunate, especially when Jesus commanded them to "wait for the promise of the Father" (Acts 1:4), and He subsequently promised them, "But ye shall receive power, after that the Holy Ghost is come upon you: and ye shall be witnesses unto me both in Jerusalem, and in all Judaea, and in Samaria, and unto the uttermost part of the earth" (Acts 1:8). Is it any wonder that churches around the world are being utterly defeated! This is because of a total disregard and lack of dependence upon the Holy Spirit's ministry. The prophet Zechariah expresses that the strength and victory of the people of God will not be by their own might or power, "but by my spirit, saith the LORD of hosts" (Zechariah 4:6).

The Mighty Man

> *"Except the LORD build the house, they labour in vain that build it: except the LORD keep the city, the watchman waketh but in vain. It is vain for you to rise up early, to sit up late, to eat the bread of sorrows: for so he giveth his beloved sleep. Lo, children are an heritage of the LORD: and the fruit of the womb is his reward. As arrows are in the hand of a mighty man; so are children of the youth Happy is the man that hath his quiver full of them: they shall not be ashamed, but they shall speak with the enemies in the gate."*
> Psalms 127 (KJV)

Psalms 127 depicts the LORD as the house Builder, Keeper of the city, and the Mighty Man whose quiver is full of arrows. More specifically, the Mighty Man portrays the Lord as a skillful archer and the arrows in His quiver (arrow carrier) as the children of God.

The Arrows

Isaiah the prophet describes himself as an arrow when he proclaims, "And he hath made my mouth like a sharp sword; in the shadow of his hand hath he hid me, and made me a polished shaft (arrow); in his quiver hath he hid me…" (Isaiah 49:2). When the Lord (the Archer) asked, "Whom shall I send (shoot), and who will go for us?" Isaiah replied, "(KJV) Here am I (the arrow); send (shoot) me" (Isaiah 6:8). Like Isaiah, the arrows are the sending of the children of God to hit the target and accomplish the Great Commission: "Go then and make disciples of all the nations…" (Matthew 28:19a AMPC). The Archer also sends us as arrows by way of "supplications, prayers, and intercessions," according to 1 Timothy 21:1, because "For this is good and acceptable in the sight of God our Saviour; 4 Who will have all men to be saved, and to come unto the knowledge of the truth" (1 Timothy 2:3-4).

The Bible says, "Yea, he sent out his arrows, and scattered them; and he shot out lightnings, and discomfited them" (Psalm 18:14). "But God shall shoot at them with an arrow; suddenly shall they be wounded" (Psalms 64:7). In the book of Zechariah, the prophet writes, "And the LORD shall be seen over them, and his arrow shall go forth as the lightning…" (Zechariah 9:14a). These and other scriptural references characterize God's children as arrows, who the Almighty Archer sends to accomplish His will on the earth.

The arrows are useless without a bow. Quite frankly, an arrow is incapable of fulfilling its intended purpose apart from a bow. It is too light and too short to be thrown like a spear and insufficient for short distances like a dark or knife. Separate from the bow, the arrow is ineffective, and therefore, the Archer cannot strike the mark, much less hit the "bullseye."

The Bow

In 2 Samuel 1:17-27, David laments the loss of those he considered mighty men of war, King Saul and his friend Jonathan, the king's son, declaring, "How are the mighty fallen!" (Verse 19); "How are the mighty fallen in the midst of the battle?" (Verse 25); and "How are the mighty fallen, and the weapons of war perished!" (Verse 27). David gives us insight into the reason for the demise of these mighty men when he declares in Verse 18, "Teach the children of Judah the use of the bow." What led to the fall of these mighty men? They no longer depended upon the Bow for their strength. The same can be said of the mighty men and women today. Without the Bow, arrows are ineffective, and the mighty fall in the midst of battle.

The Bow represents the awesome power and strength of the Holy Spirit. When we depend upon, cooperate with, and follow His lead, He empowers us to carry out the will and plan of God. Jesus did not do anything until He received the power of the Bow. He began His ministry by saying, "The Spirit of the Lord is upon me, because he hath anointed me to preach the gospel to the poor; he hath sent me to heal the brokenhearted, to preach deliverance to the captives, and recovering of sight to the blind, to set at liberty them that are bruised..." (Luke 4:18). He then declared that we would do even greater things (John 14:12) after receiving the power of the Holy Ghost (Acts 1:8). Using the Bow, the Almighty Archer takes His arrows, aims us at targets, and hits the bullseye every time. When this happens, no one praises the arrows but declares, as Frances Jane "Fanny" Crosby declared in the hymn "Brightest and Best," "To God be the Glory for the things He has done!"

Gifts of the Holy Ghost

> *"God also bearing them witness, both with signs and wonders, and with divers miracles, and gifts of the Holy Ghost, according to his own will."*
> HEBREWS 2:4 (KJV)

In Hebrews 2:4, The word *gifts* is not the same as the manifestation gifts found in 1 Corinthians 12, i.e., word of knowledge, gift of faith, gifts of healing, etc., which are known as the "gifts of the Spirit." The word for *gifts* is the Greek word *merismos*, which is recorded twice in Scripture in the book of Hebrews. In Hebrews 4:12, this same Greek word is translated from the phrase *dividing asunder*.

Merismos is a compound word of *merizo*, meaning "to separate, disunite, or take part) and *meros*, meaning "to divide into allotments and shares or to allocate." It implies that the Holy Spirit merismos Himself or divides Himself into allotments and shares. In other words, the Holy Spirit allocates Himself within the body of Christ in myriad of ways. Better yet, His ministry is identified by several functions or operations that I will briefly list. Be advised that I am not saying these are the only operations or functions of the Holy Spirit, but I will discuss ten delineated and verifiable in the Scriptures.

The following is a list of ten functions or operations of the Holy Spirit as recorded in the Scriptures:

1 | The Seal of the Spirit (Sphragizō)

> "In whom ye also trusted, after that ye heard the word of truth, the gospel of your salvation: in whom also after that ye believed, ye were sealed with that Holy Spirit of promise...."
>
> EPHESIANS 1:13 (KJV)

When we are "born again" or "born of the Spirit" (John 3:1-8), the Holy Spirit comes to live in our hearts, and we become "new creatures" (2 Corinthians 5:17). We receive the seal or "birthmark" of the Spirit, identifying us as children of God. In 2 Timothy 2:19a, Paul declares, "Nevertheless the foundation of God stands sure, having this seal, The Lord knoweth them that are his." If you are saved, you have a seal or the birthmark of the Spirit.

2 | Filled with the Spirit (Pleroo)

> "And they were all filled with the Holy Ghost, and began to speak with other tongues, as the Spirit gave them utterance."
>
> ACTS 2:4 (KJV)

When we are born of the Spirit, He comes to live inside and bears witness that we are children of God (Romans 8:16). However, now that He is in us, He wants to fill our lives and flow out of us as recorded in John 7:38-39, "He that believeth on me, as the scripture hath said, out of his belly shall flow rivers of living water. But this spake he of the Spirit, which they that believe on him should receive: for the Holy Ghost was not yet given; because that Jesus was not yet glorified.)" The flow of living water symbolizes speaking in tongues, the initial evidence of being filled with the Holy Spirit. Like a river, the flow should be continuous to remain filled (Ephesians 5:18). Therefore, praying daily in the Spirit is strongly encouraged.

3 | Baptized with the Spirit (Baptizō)

> *"For John truly baptized with water; but ye shall be baptized with the Holy Ghost not many days hence."*
>
> Acts 1:5 (KJV)

Baptized or *baptizō* means "to dip into, submerge, immerse or bury." As with all biblical baptisms, the candidate (believer) is baptized into the element, which, in this case, is the Holy Ghost. Jesus determined this baptism was critically important and commanded the disciples to wait for this experience before witnessing or ministering. Please refer back to Chapter 3 for details concerning this baptism.

4 | The Power of the Spirit (Dunamis)

> *"But ye shall receive power, after that the Holy Ghost is come upon you: and ye shall be witnesses unto me both in Jerusalem, and in all Judaea, and in Samaria, and unto the uttermost part of the earth."*
>
> ACTS 1:8 (KJV)

The *dunamis* of the Spirit is indicative of "dynamite" or miracle-working power. This power is synonymous with the anointing. Jesus said, "The Spirit of the Lord is upon me, for He has anointed me" (Luke 4:18a). Preaching to the house of Cornelius, Peter proclaimed, "How God anointed Jesus of Nazareth with the Holy Ghost and with power: who went about doing good, and healing all that were oppressed of the devil; for God was with him" (Acts 10:38). Finally, Jesus promised each of us, "But ye shall receive power, after that the Holy Ghost is come upon you: and ye shall be witnesses unto me both in Jerusalem, and in all Judaea, and in Samaria, and unto the uttermost part of the earth" (Acts 1:8). If we are going to be effective witnesses, we need the power (*dunamis*) of the Holy Ghost.

5 | Led by the Spirit (Agō)

> *"For as many as are led by the Spirit of God, they are the sons of God."*
>
> ROMANS 8:14 (KJV)

The Lord desires that we be led by the "ago" of the Spirit and not the "ego" of our souls (mind, will, and emotions). The leading of the Holy Spirit is to follow the Spirit's conviction (John 16:8) and not the condemnation of satan (Romans 8:1), the voice of the Spirit and not the voice of strangers (John 10:3-5), and ultimately become doers of the word and not hearers only (James 2:21-25). God uses mature, obedient sons (men and women), not childish children. Sons, it is time to be led by the Holy Spirit of God.

6 | *The Help of the Spirit (Sunantilambano)*

"Likewise the Spirit also helpeth our infirmities: for we know not what we should pray for as we ought: but the Spirit itself maketh intercession for us with groanings which cannot be uttered."

ROMANS 8:26 (KJV)

The Holy Spirit wants to help or take hold together with you concerning your weaknesses or where you fall short. He wants to comfort you, teach you all things, and bring all things to your remembrance (John 14:26). As the Spirit of Truth, He will guide you into all truth and show you things to come (John 16:13). Many times, we are lost for words and don't know how or what to pray. Thus, we need the Holy Spirit's help! He is available to pray with us and through us, for He knows all things and will pray according to the perfect will of God (Romans 8:27).

7 | The Fruit of the Spirit (Karpos)

> *"But the fruit of the Spirit is love, joy, peace, longsuffering, gentleness, goodness, faithfulness, meekness, temperance: against such there is no law."*
>
> GALATIANS 5:22-23 (KJV)

Jesus declared that the ultimate desire from the Father is that we bear much fruit (John 15:8). The only way to bear fruit is to abide in Him (John 15:4). The way to abide in Him is to obey His Word (John 15:7,10). Obeying His Word is based upon our love for Him (John 15:10). We love Him because we know Him (John 15:15). Therefore, the key to life is knowing, loving, obeying, and abiding in Jesus Christ so that the fruit of the Spirit can be manifest in and through our daily lives.

8 | The Gifts of the Spirit (Charisma)

> *"Now there are diversities of gifts, but the same Spirit."*
>
> 1 CORINTHIANS 12:4 (KJV)

In 1 Corinthians 12:4, the word *gifts* is the Greek word *charisma*, which finds its root in *charis*, meaning "grace and favor." It signifies the spiritual innate ability or what a person was born to be or do. Often called the charisma gift, it is also known as the grace or motivational gift. Every person born has this gift as it is the motivating factor that makes up the personality. Paul said, "But by the grace (*charis*) of God I am what I am" (1 Corinthians 15:10). Romans 12:6-8 outlines seven motivational gifts: "Having then gifts (charisma) differing according to the grace (*charis*) that is given to us," including prophecy-motivated, server-motivated, teacher-motivated, exhorter-motivated, giver-motivated, ruler-motivated, and mercy-motivated. It is vitally important for a person to find out who they are by grace before trying to find what to do in ministry.

9 | The Manifestation of the Spirit (Phanerōsis)

> "But the manifestation of the Spirit is given to every man to profit withal."
>
> 1 Corinthians 12:7 (KJV)

There are nine manifestations of the Holy Spirit: word of wisdom, word of knowledge, the gift of faith, gifts of healing, working of miracles, prophecy, discerning of spirits, divers kinds of tongues, and the interpretation of tongues. The manifestation of the Spirit operates when the Holy Spirit decides (1 Corinthians 12:7-11), and no man controls them. These manifestations or gifts are for every man's profit or those who need them. They are never for the benefit of those through whom the gift operates, but they will always give glory to God. Therefore, the body of Christ should strive to give place to the Holy Spirit to manifest and expect them by faith on a daily basis.

10 | The Demonstration of the Spirit (Apodeixis)

> *"And my speech and my preaching was not with enticing words of man's wisdom, but in demonstration of the Spirit and of power: That your faith should not stand in the wisdom of men, but in the power of God."*
>
> 1 CORINTHIANS 2:4-5 (KJV)

Demonstration means "to prove, show forth, or display, by the operation of the Spirit of God." Here, the Holy Spirit puts on a show, or like the old folks used to say, He "shows up" and "shows out!" During military training, the instructor verbally instructed and taught lessons, and then presented a live display or visual aid and announced, "Now, watch this demonstration!" In a Holy Ghost demonstration, He does whatever He wants with little or no assistance from man. When Moses and Israel faced the Red Sea, the Spirit told him to stretch out the rod, or in essence, "Now, watch this demonstration." On Mount Carmel, He told Elijah to build an altar, fill it with water, and then told him, "Now, watch this demonstration." Empowered by the Spirit, Jesus allowed Lazarus to die, then told them to roll back the stone and "Watch this demonstration." The Holy Spirit demonstrates "That your faith should not stand in the wisdom of men, but in the power of God" (1 Corinthians 2:5).

The Church built by the Lord to carry out His will on earth must greatly depend upon the Holy Spirit's ministry, expressed in these operations and functions. People intimately acquainted with Him will take the land "not by might, nor by power, but by my spirit, saith the LORD of hosts" (Zechariah 4:6).

---

*"The presence of the Holy Spirit
is the keystone of all our hopes."*

JOHN NELSON DARBY

The Father's Anointing

9

*"And it came to pass, when they were gone over, that Elijah said unto Elisha, Ask what I shall do for thee, before I be taken away from thee. And Elisha said, I pray thee, let a **double portion** of thy spirit be upon me."*

2 Kings 2:9 (KJV) Emphasis Added

When the prophet Elisha requested the "double portion" from the prophet Elijah, he asked for the portion due to the firstborn son. In essence, Elisha was requesting what was rightfully his as the spiritual son of Elijah. Throughout the Scriptures, we find the importance of the firstborn son, who was granted twice the inheritance as the other sons. Since Elisha was not Elijah's biological son, applying this principle was of spiritual significance. Elijah delineated this principle when he went up in a whirlwind as Elisha cried, "My father, my father" (2 Kings 2:12). Verses 13 and 14 say that Elisha:

> He took up also the mantle of Elijah that fell from

him, and went back, and stood by the bank of Jordan; And he took the mantle of Elijah that fell from him, and smote the waters, and said, Where is the LORD God of Elijah? and when he also had smitten the waters, they parted hither and thither: and Elisha went over.

The son received what he asked for: the double portion of the firstborn son or the Father's anointing.

To further qualify this assertion, it is necessary to go back to the beginning of Elijah and Elisha's relationship. In 1 Kings 19:16, the Lord directs the prophet concerning kingdom appointments, saying to Elijah, "And Jehu the son of Nimshi shalt thou anoint to be king over Israel: and Elisha the son of Shaphat of Abelmeholah shalt thou anoint to be prophet in thy room." Notice that the Lord chose the replacement for the prophet Elijah. After hearing from the Lord, Verse 19 says that he departed, found Elisha working, "passed by him, and cast his mantle upon him." The Scriptures then record that Elisha "left the oxen, and ran after Elijah, and said, Let me, I pray thee, kiss my father and my mother, and then I will follow thee…" (Verse 20). Elisha left his estate, job, and family "and went after Elijah, and ministered unto him" (Verse 21). Research revealed that the period between the first meeting and the next time we hear about Elisha was seven to eight years. In other words, Elisha served under the tutelage of Elijah for close to 10 years before his release into ministry.

Picking up the narrative in 2 Kings 2, we find the process of sonship or the training that Elisha received before the transfer of the Father's anointing. In this text, the "School of the Prophets" or "the Sons of the Prophets" prepared for their father-teacher to leave them. Yet, Elisha followed Elijah from Gilgal to Bethel to Jericho and finally to Jordan. Let me point out that the other sons of the prophets only followed him as far as the place where they were, but only Elisha went all the way to Jordan. For the sake of being point blank, the journey from Gilgal to Jordan outlines the preparation afforded Elisha to develop into a mature son.

First, he went to Gilgal, which means covenant, circle, or ring. In Gilgal, Elisha receives the promise of his calling. Gilgal represents the place of starting, where Elisha receives the first principle or basic fundamental teachings from the Word of God. Secondly, Elisha went to Bethel, which stands for the house of God or the church. In Bethel, the place of serving, Elisha learned to serve in the church. Thirdly, he followed on to Jericho, which represents pressure or conflict. In Jericho, the place of struggling or doing battle, Elisha learns how to endure afflictions and persecutions and not lose His faith in God. Finally, Elisha crossed the Jordan, which denotes a "crossing over" or promotion. At the Jordan, the place of separation into the calling, he received the anointing.

In sum, upon crossing the Jordan and after his father's departure,

Elisha was granted the double portion of the anointing due to a son. Later, when the sons of the prophets saw him, they bore witness, saying, "The spirit of Elijah doth rest on Elisha. And they came to meet him, and bowed themselves to the ground before him" (2 Kings 2:15). There was such an agreement in the spirit of the other sons that they gave reverence to Elisha and now received him as their father. The Scriptures record that Elisha went on to perform twice as many miracles as Elijah because of the double portion anointing that came from his father.

The Spiritual Father

> *"I write not these things to shame you, but as my beloved sons I warn you. For though ye have ten thousand instructors in Christ, yet have ye not many fathers: for in Christ Jesus I have begotten you through the gospel."*
> 1 CORINTHIANS 4:14-15 (KJV)

Verse 15b in the *Amplified Bible, Classic Edition*, says, "For I became your father in Christ Jesus through the glad tidings (the Gospel)," which refers to "father in the faith." To the well-meaning people who say there is no biblical reference for spiritual fathers or fathers in the faith, I submit to you that the *Vines Expository Dictionary* defines this text as such: "of one who, as a preacher of the Gospel and a teacher, stands in a father's place, caring for his spiritual children." *Vines* goes on to say that this is not for mere title, as prohibited by the Lord, but these spiritual fathers are to care for the sons just like the Lord Himself. Paul concludes in Verse 17, "For this cause have I sent unto you Timotheus (Timothy), who is my beloved son, and faithful in the Lord, who shall bring you into remembrance of my ways which be in Christ, as I teach everywhere in every church." To Timothy, a young pastor, Paul, in his writing to him, refers to him as his son. Thus, we derive the concept of spiritual father or father in the faith.

Like Father, Like Son

In the book of First John, the apostle sends a letter addressing three classes: little children, young men, and fathers (1 John 2:12-14). This indicates that we need fathers to cause the children to become young men and eventually fathers. While I am not saying that this applies in every instance, in most cases, these fathers are found in the person of an apostle or bishop. Again. I am not saying that a father has to be identified with one of these titles. However, apostles and bishops provide doctrinal teaching and covering for sons. Also, titles serve as identification for the anointing, not as a prestigious tag. Many men and women don't necessarily wear the title of apostle or bishop but possess the anointing of a father.

Seeing some functioning in ministry without any spiritual connection to a father is a shame. No accountability or anyone of experience can vouch for and bear witness to the calling and separation concerning their work. I call these fathers "checkers," those who have the insight for oversight and provide counsel, correction, and instruction to the sons. Furthermore, Paul directed Timothy to bring the church at Corinth "into remembrance of my ways which be in Christ, as I teach everywhere in every church" (1 Corinthians 4:17b). Paul encouraged Timothy to preach and teach the same word he preached and taught. In other words, "speak the same thing" (1 Corinthians 1:10). A better way of saying it is, "Like father, like son!"

The Prodigal Son

The parable of the prodigal son found in the Gospel of Luke 15 illustrates a son leaving without the father's anointing and, ultimately, his blessing. The story begins in Verse 11 by saying, "A certain man had two sons," referred to as the younger son and the elder son. The younger son asked the father for the portion due to him. He then took his inheritance and journeyed to a far country. Note that the younger son did not get his father's blessing to signify that he was trained, prepared, and mature enough to be separated to function on his own. Thus, the younger son squandered his inheritance with wild living and ended up in the "hog-pen" or the "gutter" of life.

Eventually, he came to himself and realized that he had it better in his father's house or under the covering and protection of his father. The younger son quickly arose, returned to his father, and found him waiting for his return with open arms. The father restored him to his place of sonship and put on a huge celebration.

In the meantime, the elder son was not home when his brother returned home. So, when the elder son returned home, he heard the noise from the party and asked one of the servants what was happening. When the servant informed him that his father was celebrating his younger brother's return, he angrily refused to attend the party. When his father heard about it and went out to see what was wrong, the elder son said, "All these years I served you and you never threw me a party" (Verse 29). The father responded, "Son, thou are ever with me, and all that I have is thine." I am celebrating because your "brother was dead, and is alive again; and was lost and is found" (Verses 31-32).

Two lessons can be learned from these two sons. First, the younger son was disconnected and separated from the father too soon. He did not allow the full process of sonship to take place and, therefore, departed without the father's blessing. Second, the elder son was discouraged and stayed too long. He had been with the father long enough that he should have had the father's spirit and been excited over what the father was excited about. Also, He should have been preparing to eventually depart from the father with the full blessing of the double portion. Neither of these sons embodied the characteristics of a mature son developed to receive the inheritance of the father's anointing.

I pray that every minister reading this book would endeavor to get and stay connected to a spiritual father who can consistently do as Paul said in Romans 1:11, "For I long to see you, that I may impart unto you some spiritual gift to the end ye may be established." Fathers in the faith are given unto us by our Heavenly Father to raise us, train us, impart into us, and help develop us into mature sons, who will be as Paul said unto his son Timothy: "Thou therefore my son, be strong in the grace that is Christ Jesus. And the things that thou has heard of me among many witnesses, the same commit thou to faithful men, who shall be able to teach others also" (2 Timothy 2:1-2). We need fathers so that we can grow into mature sons and receive the Father's Anointing!

"Even if you had ten thousand guardians in Christ, you do not have many fathers, for in Christ Jesus I became your father through the gospel."

1 CORINTHIANS 4:15 NIV

The Mighty Hand of God

10

"Humble yourself therefore under the mighty hand of God, that he may exalt you in due time."

1 Peter 5:6

Ephesians 4:11 says, "And he gave some, apostles; and some, prophets; and some, evangelists; and some, pastors and teachers." In this text of scripture, we find what is commonly known as the 5-fold Ministry—also referred to as the Ministry Gifts. These five are widely considered the Government of God for the Church. Before delving into each of these positions in more detail, I would like to point out that in Jesus, we see all five personified. Jesus is considered the Apostle and High Priest of our profession (Hebrew 3:1); the Prophet like unto Moses (Acts 3:22); He came to seek and save the lost as the ultimate Evangelist (Luke 19:10); He declares Himself the Good Shepherd or Pastor (John 10:10); and He's known as the Teacher that comes from God (John 3:2). While we can see that He embodied the ministry gifts, I must point out that Jesus epitomized the Model Servant.

Servant-Leaders

While far too many consider these as glamorous positions and levels of grandeur, Jesus made it very clear that the greatest in the kingdom is to be the servant of all. Speaking to the disciples and future apostles, Jesus said, "Whoever wants to be a leader among you must be your servant" (Matthew 20:26 NLT). The prevailing fallacy held among many in the church is that leaders are above the members and, therefore, are esteemed as great, but this was never the will of God for church leadership. While washing the disciple's feet, Jesus set the perfect example. He proclaimed to them, "If I, your Lord and teacher, have washed your feet, you too must wash each other's feet. I have given you an example: Just as I have done, you also must do" (John 13:14-15 CEB). The apostle Peter captured the essence of the servant-leader when he directed the elders to "Like shepherds, tend the flock of God among you. Watch over it. Don't shepherd because you must, but do it voluntarily for God. Don't shepherd greedily, but do it eagerly. Don't shepherd by ruling over those entrusted to your care, but become examples to the flock" (1 Peter 5:2-3 CEB).

The Highest Call of All

Contrary to popular belief, the highest call in the Bible is not the heavenly calling of salvation (Hebrews 3:1), the holy calling of sanctification (2 Timothy 1:9), or the calling of any one of the five ministry gifts. This may surprise some, but the highest call is found in Philippians 3:14, where you "press toward the mark for the prize of the high calling of God in Christ Jesus." Thus, the highest call is to be a servant, as illustrated by Jesus Himself. Much like our Lord, this will require the servant-leader to have a heart of humility and the spirit of submission. This adage holds true: "A good leader must be a good follower first." This is true not just in church but in every area of life.

A Heart of Humility

A humble heart is a prerequisite of the servant-leader, as the apostle James declares, "God resists the proud, but gives more grace to the humble" (James 4:6). This bespeaks of the heart or the spirit in man that causes him/her to be humble. In the world, most leaders are selected and appointed by outward appearance, physical attributes, and mental prowess. For instance, the account of young David anointed as king of Israel fits this example. As Jesse paraded all of his sons before Samuel, God said about each of them, "Do not look at his appearance or at the height of his stature, because I have rejected him; for God sees not as man sees, for man looks at the outward appearance, but the LORD looks at the heart" (1 Samuel 16:7 NASB).

The heart of humility or to be humble means to lower yourself in your own estimation. It carries the connotation that you must do it on purpose because no one can do it for you or make you do it. God made every person a free moral agent with a soul (mind, will, and emotions); a humble heart will always produce the fruit of submission, and your will is yours to submit. So to all servant-leaders, the Lord says, "Humble yourselves in the sight of the Lord, and he shall lift you up" (James 4:10).

The Spirit of Submission

In simple terms, submission is to be sub or under the mission. It means to subordinate or subject yourself willfully and intentionally. Submission and humility are interchangeable terms, but humility is the heart that provokes the act of submission. Similar to humbling yourself, no one can force you to submit. Submission is your choice every time, in every situation and every circumstance. The late Apostle Nate Holcomb always said, "Submission is according to your own will and not based upon an emotion of how you feel." Therefore, authentic leadership is not an act of domination or superiority but submission by cooperation from a heart of humility. It's important to point out that the fruit of submission is obedience. If someone truly submits, it will result in willful obedience. So, servant-leaders, the Lord says, "Submit yourselves therefore unto God. Resist the devil, and he will flee from you" (James 4:7).

The 5-Fold Hand of Ministry

God's right hand is a phrase used throughout the Scriptures to denote His power and authority. According to Hebrews 12:2, Jesus "sat down at the right hand of the throne of God." This symbolizes equal honor and indicates that Jesus possesses the same authority. After the resurrection and before His ascension, Jesus declared, "All authority has been given to me in heaven and on earth" (Matthew 28:18). Now, as members of the Body of Christ, we have been delegated power and authority in Jesus' name. I will now use the fingers of the human hand to delineate the members of the 5-fold Ministry who have delegated authority to oversee specific areas of the ministry.

Apostle (The Thumb)

The thumb identifies the apostle. Like the thumb, the only finger that easily touches all the others, the apostle can release all the other members into ministry. An apostle is defined as a "messenger or one sent forth." Interchangeable with a missionary, an apostle is "one who is sent and commissioned with the task of founding and establishing churches, ministries and movements." A common misconception is that the apostle and bishop are the same. This mistaken belief is inaccurate because an apostle is a church planter, and a bishop is an overseer of a church. For example, the apostle Paul established more than eight churches and ordained elders to oversee them. Apostles are not only sent to plant churches but also to ensure they are established on the Apostle's Doctrine (Acts 2:42) that centers around the preaching of Jesus Christ and the sound teaching of fundamentals that foster believer's maturity and spiritual growth. In sum, every local church should be established under the auspices of an apostle.

Prophet (The Index Finger)

The index finger identifies the prophet's ministry. Prophets are widely known as "Seers" who foretell the future, but their primary function is to carry God's Word to His people. Prophets are inspired teachers and preachers according to the will of God. They possess a unique gift of prophecy to provide correction and protection to point the church in the right direction. They possess the innate ability and sensitivity to God's Word for particular seasons and situations and the unique anointing to recognize the gifts and calling of God for others in the body of Christ. Prophets often provide counsel and guidance to others in the church.

Correction for Protection

The true essence of a prophet is found in 1 Corinthians 14:3, "But he that prophesieth speaketh unto men to edification, exhortation, and comfort." A prophet corrects us for our ultimate protection and to build up, encourage, and ultimately supply comfort to our souls. Prophets often judge (discern, evaluate, or weigh) spiritual matters and provide godly insight concerning God's will. The prophet Nathan was known for giving King David godly counsel and correcting the king when he had committed multiple grave sins. The prophet's ministry must be available in the local church on a regular basis.

Evangelist (Middle Finger)

Because the middle finger extends beyond the others, it represents the evangelist. Also known as the messenger, the evangelist is skilled in the outreach ministry. This consummate soul winner primarily functions outside the church, proclaiming the gospel. The Oxford Dictionary defines an evangelist as "One who seeks to convert others to the Christian faith, especially by public preaching." While every Christian and follower of Christ is charged to evangelize those outside the body of Christ, the evangelist has a passion and is particularly strong in preaching and witnessing so that sinners are saved and ultimately become disciples of Jesus Christ.

The Work of an Evangelist

According to Matthew 28:19 (CEB), Jesus commands every disciple to "therefore, go and make disciples of all nations." Paul further directs that all ministers "do the work of an evangelist" in 2 Timothy 4:5. The principal purpose is that every Christian follower is under orders to be a star witness, intending to convert sinners to Jesus Christ. A perfect picture of this in action is found in the Book of Acts, Chapter 8, Verse 4. The *Amplified Bible* version of this text reads, "Now those [believers] who had been scattered went from place to place preaching the word [the good news of salvation through Christ]." Commonly known as the Great Commission for our Lord, while every Christian is given this directive, only the evangelist possesses it as a gift.

The Gift of an Evangelist

There is a vast difference between the command to do the work of an evangelist and the calling and gift of an evangelist. The anointing that the evangelists have enables them to naturally and comfortably share the good news of Jesus Christ anytime, anywhere, and with anybody. A bona fide evangelist is well known for traveling from place to place and preaching in churches and arenas. They are the primary organizers and facilitators of spiritual revivals and other outdoor events to propagate the preaching of the Good News. The quintessential model of the gifted evangelist is found in Phillip the

Evangelist, mentioned several times in the Acts of the Apostles. Phillip is known for his passionate evangelism: He is ultimately responsible for a eunuch and unbeliever receiving Jesus Christ and being baptized. According to Acts 8:35, "Phillip opened his mouth, and began at the same scripture, and preached unto him Jesus." As a result of Phillip's preaching, the eunuch replied, "I believe that Jesus Christ is the Son of God" (Verse 37), and Phillip baptized him in water. A gifted evangelist like Phillip must lead the way if the church is to fulfill the Great Commission.

Pastor (The Ring Finger)

Just as the ring finger symbolizes loyalty in marriage, the pastor has an altruistic commitment to the congregation. Now, it is necessary to point out that only Jesus is married to the church, not the pastors. However, as the ring remains on the ring finger, the pastor displays an unwavering allegiance to the local church. Most Christians are well aware that the word *pastor* means "shepherd," but it is vital to understand that Jesus is the lone Shepherd of the church-flock; pastors are "under-shepherds" or shepherds under the Shepherd. The pastoral ministry includes feeding and leading, correcting and protecting, and developing the members of the church-flock. The pastoral ministry cannot be overemphasized, as pastors are spiritual caregivers who are primarily responsible for the sustenance, growth, guidance and safety of the members of the congregations.

Teacher (The Pinky)

Like the little finger or "the pinky" that gives balance to the hand, the teacher brings balance to the body of Christ through sound and wholesome teaching of the Word of God. The Greek word for *teach* is *Didasko*, which means "to teach knowledge, instruct, inform, and ultimately develop" the people of God in the Word. Teachers undoubtedly have an uncanny ability to simplify and clarify things using detailed explanations and illustrations. They are given to the facts and the study of findings. Although all members of the 5-fold Ministry are called to preach and teach the Word of God, the teacher has a unique gift to break down and share the full counsel of God. The truth is that there is a distinct difference between the gospel and God's full counsel, which I will now discuss in more detail.

Preach the Gospel

The true nature of the Gospel can be stated in one particular verse of Scripture, "For God so loved the world, that he gave his only begotten Son, that whosoever believeth in him should not perish, but have everlasting life" (John 3:16). In simplest terms, the Good News is that Jesus died on Calvary's cross for the sins of the whole world, and believing and receiving Him is the only way to be saved. Consequently, preaching and teaching the Gospel is the responsibility of every minister. However, after receiving the Good News and becoming a child of God, it is vitally important to learn to live according to the plan of God, as delineated in the Holy Scriptures. This is where the teacher comes in, for they are anointed to teach and preach the full counsel of God.

Teach God's Full Counsel

Paul said, "For I have not shunned to declare unto you all the counsel of God" (Acts 20:27). As mentioned before, there is a vast difference between the preaching of the Gospel and the teaching of God's counsel. The Gospel is about the plan of salvation, but the counsel encompasses God's promises and His will and purpose for every area of life. Furthermore, the counsel includes, but is not limited to, such things as the principles of faith, healing and deliverance, righteousness, the love of God, prayer, identity in Christ, marriage, and living single (to name a few). Jesus is the epitome of an anointed teacher, and he captured the essence of God's counsel when he declared, "I came that they may have and enjoy life, and have it in abundance [to the full, till it overflows]" (John 10:10 AMPC). After getting saved, we need gifted teachers to help develop us to live the lives God promised and intended all along, according to His full counsel.

Bishop (Overseer)

Right from the outset, let me start by saying I am not trying to discredit the ministry of the bishop, nor am I trying to disrespect those functioning as bishops. I deeply and sincerely respect bishops and all spiritual leaders in Christ's body. I aim to dispel the false notion that bishop and apostle are synonymous terms and show that this is incorrect according to the Bible and nothing more than a misunderstanding.

Bishop Defined

The bishop is not an apostle and, therefore, not listed as part of the 5-fold Ministry. Much of the misinterpretation of the bishop derives from an inaccurate explanation of 1 Timothy 3:1, which reads, "This is a true saying, if a man desires the *office of* a bishop, he desires a good work." It is also important to point out that "office of" is italicized because it does not appear in the original text and was added later. Furthermore, only two versions of the Bible use the term bishop, and all others, including the original writings, translate this as an *overseer*. The Greek word for *bishop* is *episkopos*, meaning "overseer, superintendent, and elder." In Greek terms, *bishop, elder* and *presbyter* are synonymous. It denotes a senior Christian clergy member overseeing one or more churches.

First Timothy 3:1-13 outlines the qualifications of what we

consider as church leaders but only delineates the overseer and deacons. It does not mention apostles, prophets, evangelists, pastors, or teachers because the overseer or elder includes all of the members of the 5-fold Ministry. Speaking to other elders, the apostle Peter captured this when he said, "Therefore, I strongly urge the elders among you [pastors, spiritual leaders of the church], as a fellow elder]" (1 Peter 5:1 AMPC).

Bishop's Duties

The word *manager* gives a good summation and explanation of the duty and responsibility of a bishop. The bishop is a spiritual manager who oversees others spiritually or ecclesiastically. Bishops are responsible for governing and the overall administration of a church or several churches. In Titus 1:5, the apostle Paul provides the basic duties of the *bishop* or *overseer*, saying, "The reason I left you in Crete was that you might put in order what was left unfinished and appoint elders in every town, as I directed you."

In sum, the 5-fold Ministry Gifts, as illustrated by the human hand, are essential for the church's spiritual health and ultimate growth. It will do us good to identify and submit ourselves to God's purpose for giving these five gifts as found in Ephesians 4:12 AMPC, "[and He did this] to fully equip and perfect the saints (God's people) for works of service, to build up the body of Christ (the church)."

SHOW THE HOUSE TO THE HOUSE

"True leadership is found in giving yourself in service to others, not in coaxing or inducing others to serve you."

J. OSWALD SANDERS

About the Author

Dr. Vernon L. Fowler serves as the pastor of Dominion Church and is a renowned inspirational speaker.

As the pastor, his mandate is to focus everything and everybody upon Jesus Christ by committing himself and the ministry to pray about everything. He is fully persuaded that God has called him according to Luke 4:18-19, "The Spirit of the Lord is upon me, because he has anointed me to preach the gospel to the poor; He hath sent me to heal the brokenhearted, to preach deliverance to the captives, and recovering of sight to the blind, to set at liberty them that are bruised, and to preach the acceptable year (coming) of the Lord."

Dr. Fowler diligently teaches that ministry begins at home and endeavors to build and strengthen the "total family." He preaches a message of family unity, which leads to church unity, and that is where the blessing of God is.

Dr. Fowler retired from the U.S. Army in 2004 with 23 years of military service. He served in various assignments and leadership positions, which culminated in him being a First Sergeant. He completed an illustrious military career as a highly decorated soldier and continues to serve military members and their families.

Dr. Vernon Fowler has been a devoted husband for over 37 years, a dedicated father and grandfather, and a disciplined undershepherd with a servant's heart. He serves with his beautiful wife, First Lady Tracy O. Fowler.

www.ingramcontent.com/pod-product-compliance
Lightning Source LLC
Chambersburg PA
CBHW050639160426
43194CB00010B/1731